NIGHT
MOVEMENTS

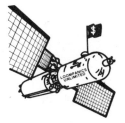

Loompanics Unlimited
Port Townsend, Washington

Published by:
Loompanics Unlimited
PO Box 1197
Port Townsend, WA 98368

ISBN 0-915179-79-2

Library of Congress
    Card Catalog Number 88-045200

NIGHT MOVEMENTS

Translated From The Japanese

by
C. Burnett

TRANSLATOR'S PREFACE.

The importance of night movements and night attacks in the military operations of the present day is so generally recognized, that any discussion on that point would be more than superfluous. That the Japanese army, from the standpoint of practical experience, is best qualified to discuss such operations, would seem to follow as a matter also beyond discussion. For this reason it occured to me that the translation of this work of a Japanese officer who was a company commander during the Japanese-Russian War, might, and I venture to say, does contain much that will be of interest and profit to our own service.

Night movements are admittedly among the most difficult operations of war; the margin between victory and defeat is so small that it is a difficult matter to say to just what comparatively trivial reason success or failure may be due. Such being the case, it naturally follows that minute and painstaking training is absolutely necessary if success can be even hoped for. Military writers on this subject have usually recognized that fact, but their treatment of the matter has consisted so largely of vague generalities that they are not of much assistance to Captain Jones in the training of his company and are absolutely useless to Sergeant Smith in leading his squad. This work is not an academic discussion of night movements in general, but is full of valuable practical hints on the training of the small units that go to make up the great military machine; hints not evolved from the inner consciousness, but ideas stamped in the mind by actual experiences of nights on Manchurian battlefields.

Due perhaps to national characteristics, Japanese army training of all kinds proceeds along more exact and minute lines than is usual in our own service. While many may consider that this work errs in that direction, it would be well to consider carefully the necessity for such careful training in the most delicate of all military movements. If Private Brown has not been thoroughly trained and accustomed to night movements, he is sure to make mistakes; multiply him by a hundred or a thousand, and the margin of safety for success will become rather slim, to say the least.

This work has been translated at odd times in the press of much other work of the same general character. For this reason there has been no time to spend on niceties of expression or in polishing up the English; and indeed I am not sure but that following the author's words rather closely does not more than compensate for faulty diction. If the meaning can be comprehended I shall be satisfied and beg indulgence for all the things lacking.

Tokyo, Japan.

October, 1913.

CONTENTS.

6

TRAINING IN NIGHT MOVEMENTS

BASED ON

ACTUAL EXPERIENCES IN WAR

I.

PSYCHOLOGICAL ACTION AT NIGHTTIME.

From an educational standpoint, a thorough knowledge of psychological processes at night is a most important matter, because the weightiest considerations in night movements are mental ones. Therefore, I will explain this matter at the very beginning.

Having seen a thing with my own eyes, I can form my judgment concerning it; by knowing that there is no danger to my own body, I will be calm. On account of my being calm, there will be no uncertainty; on account of there being no uncertainty, all things, necessarily, will be clear. In order that there may be that clearness, a broad field of view and a clear understanding of facts are necessary. However, at nighttime, a person is not able to see his surroundings; accordingly it is only natural that there should be uncertainty. One cannot know when there will be danger in the darkness just a little ways ahead. In such cases there is a feeling of apprehension, of doubt and uncertainty, and finally there is extremely cautious watchfulness and fear. In short, at nighttime, the mind is agitated and excited.

Night and Morbid Watchfulness.—Attention is the term applied to a condition of affairs when the consciousness is concentrated on certain substances or certain ideas. At night, as the field of view is very limited, great attention must be paid to the multitude of surrounding objects; if this is not done, one will quickly fall into danger. In the presence of the enemy, how much more must the amount of watchfulness, on account of its relation to life and death, give rise to the greatest of care—and one becomes unable to distinguish between fact and fancy. As a result of too much care and concentration, what has hitherto been imagination almost ceases to be such, and approaches reality. The imagination is so vivid that unreal things seem real.

Night and Illusions.—At night, illusion is easy; there are various kinds of such illusions, as:

1. Confusion which arises from an error of the senses.

2. An illusion which forms a mistaken impression through not having made a proper impression on the senses.

3. An illsuion arising entirely from confusion of mind.

At nighttime, illsuions very often arise. For example, white clothes hanging on willow trees, or white flags in a cemetery, become ghosts; an old rope in the grasss seems a snake; tall pillars, or bundles of Manchurian millet, an enemy, etc.

In the presence of the enemy, such illusions are dangerous.

At Night, Suggestion is Easy.—Whenever the mind is agitated, the nerves also become keen. Insignificant causes, also, have the power to suggest things quickly. These suggestions are of various kinds—imitative, inductive, synchronic, etc. On account of such suggestions, confusion, mistakes, false reports, etc., in one detachment, will extend quickly to the entire body. On this account there are not a few examples where a single soldier at nighttime, who fancied that he saw an enemy, quickly gave the whole force the impression that there was, in reality, an enemy present. Again, if one person unexpectedly lays down, or halts, those accompanying him, not understanding the reason for his action, in their uncertainty, do the same. Did not such a thing cause the rout of the Heishi clan at Fushigawa?

At first, probably hearing the noise of a flying bird and thinking it was the enemy, the movement or cry of a single man extended to the whole army. During the Japanese-Russian War, a detachment of the Russian army in a seacoast fortification was thrown into disorder on account of one or two men in front crying out that there was a night attack, thereby causing the whole force to fall into disorder.

Night Brings out the Weak Points of the Individual.— A state of uncertainty at night gives rise to the idea of danger; from this there develops a state of fear. Mankind, in crowds, has an excessive mental action. That is, a crowd is conscious of vast power; hence, certain movements, though difficult for the individual, will be bravely carried out by several men together. While one man is fearful and uncertain, a number of men together, will enter into the movement almost without consideration. Therefore, at night, although one man, alone, will be afraid, several together will show no indecision whatever. This fact should be borne in mind in all night movements.

In the matter of mental phenomena, the man who has weak points in the daytime will be spurred on by vanity, love of fame, or perhaps by a self-denying spirit; but when night comes, on account of the lack or the slackness of supervision of his officers and comrades, the individual weakness will quickly show. It is not a good thing to leave the individual without supervision at night, neither is it a good thing to place him in such circumstances as will bring out these weaknesses.

II.

IMPORTANT MEASURES WHICH CORRECT UNFAVORABLE
PSYCHOLOGICAL ACTION AT NIGHT.

Although nighttime has the disadvantages mentioned above, there will be times when it will be absolutely necessary to employ soldiers individually. It is, therefore, necessary to train them so that the evils due to fits of characteristic weaknesses will never arise.

At Night, Especially, Strict Discipline is Necessary.—Nighttime is the touchstone which determines the value of an army. As supervision is difficult, strict discipline is necessary. The greatest influence of discipline is to repress the weaknesses which grow out of individuality, and to prevent the expression of those weaknesses. An army which does not have good discipline at night, will completely fall to pieces. If the individual is allowed to follow his own desires, an army is ruined. Therefore, successful night operations demand the strictest discipline; it is such discipline that spurs night operations to success.

A High Morale and a Firm Offensive Spirit.—Mental agitation depends upon the state of morale. If the morale be high, there will be no such agitation; therefore, the evils, *i. e.*, the mental phenomena previously described, will not arise. In general, a negative mind always acts unfavorably; therefore, in the case of individuals whose morale is low and who are negative in principle, the following psychological action will arise:

1. A morbid watchfulness.
2. Illusions.
3. Suggestions.
4. Weak points of individual character.

Therefore, a high morale is necessarily required to successfully overcome such weaknesses. As a matter of fact, a high morale is the foundation of successful night operations. A person with a high morale does not stand by passively, but acts, perhaps unconsciously, in a positive manner.

Silence in Night Movements.—Silence causes an agitated mind to become cool; on the contrary, disorder causes more confusion. Although, at times, it is both a material and abstract advantage to powerfully excite a man in order to drive him toward a certain objective, the importance of maintaining silence at night, must not be lost sight of. There are, naturally, two reasons for this, viz:

1. In order not to be discovered by the enemy.
2. In order to avoid falling into confusion, yourself.

At night, as it is impossible to discriminate by sight, judgment must be formed from the sounds heard. However, in what way will an ordinary sound which arises in one detachment, be transmitted to others, especially in the case of those detachments who hear this disquieting sound and already believe themselves in danger?

Therefore, at night, in order not to be discovered by the enemy, as well as to prevent falling into disorder, yourself, it is absolutely necessary to remain quiet.

Night and Massed Formation.—On account of its large numbers, great things can be accomplished with a massed force; for the self-consciousness of great strength causes great energy. At night, a large massed force destroys those individual characteristics, the various evils of which I have already clearly explained. On account of the difficulty of leadership, communication and contact, confusion and separation are easy. From a psychological standpoint, as well, it is advantageous to avoid the distribution of columns, and to use the close columns instead. A brave, determined advance is of special importance in night movements.

Night Movements and Self-confidence.—Self-confidence is the foundation of bravery; it is the requisite of a high morale. If one wishes to obtain self-confidence, there must be no indecision; in order that there may be no indecision, there must be no obscurity. Therefore it follows that conditions should be clearly understood, and that we become rich in experience. That is the reason why thoroughness of reconnaissance, observation, and training are particularly necessary for night movements. If the state of the enemy as well as the terrain be well known, and if the troops be well trained in night movements, there will be no indecision, and the movement can be carried out by methods and means which may be deemed best. A thing carried out in the belief that success is certain, will be carried out in a recklessly brave manner; that is the reason for the necessity of self-confidence at night.

Night Movements and Self-possession.—At night, one cannot tell at what distance or at what time there will be personal danger. If the enemy be heard, the danger seems the same whether he be a hundred, or only ten paces away. Therefore, a person of negative spirit feels the enemy pressing upon him, even though in reality, he is far away; and an imaginary enemy becomes the same as a real one. Therefore, in order not to make rash and disorderly movements, causes must be judged cooly.

III.

HOW TO DRESS.

The Requirements of Dress.—Dress must conform to the following requirements:

1. Speed.
2. Propriety.
3. Reliability.

To carry out these requirements, training is necessary. It is a bad thing to attach too great weight to speed at first, and make light of propriety and reliability. Therefore, at first, the following requirements must be observed:

1. Do not demand useless rapidity, but rather coolness.

2. Proper arrangement.

3. As far as possible, quiteness should be preserved. The necessary things should be taken from their fixed places only when about to be put on, so as to avoid confusion.

Coolness.—More haste, less speed. If one be confused, he will mistake the proper order or forget important things, and sometimes it will be necessary to change what has already been put on.

Order.—Order is the shortest road, and if followed, there will be nothing forgotten. However hurried one may be, it is important not to curtail or change the order; therefore, it is necessary to plan carefully, the most suitable order of procedure—a practical impossibility for one without experience. For these reasons, it is a good thing to fix a suitable order of procedure, and carry it out strictly.

Quietness.—At night, quietness is very necessary, especially in the proximity of the enemy. Therefore, it is important, in time of peace, to demand quietness, and to carry out such a training that there will be no talking or noise. If the soldier has had this training, it is an easy thing to remain quiet. If he has not, it is a very difficult matter. While a sudden demand for quiet is no hardship upon persons accustomed to it, it is most irksome to those who are not so accustomed to it.

Order of Dressing.—In order that dressing may progress smoothly, a proper order is necessary. In this order, it is important that mind and hand follow natural movements. The following example of correct procedure is from my own experience:

1. Clothing, shoes and leggins will be worn and put on in the following order: socks, trousers, leggins, blouse, cap.

2. Hang haversack and water bottle over the shoulder.

3. Place the required articles in the knapsack, roll the overcoat; attach tools, spare shoes, and mess tin to the knapsack, and put it on.

4. Take the rifle in the hand (at this time, take off the muzzle cover and place it in its prescribed place).

Although there are times when this order will not be adhered to, and it will be necessary to arrange the clothing so as to take rifle and ammunition first, the habit of handling these articles in their proper order in time of peace is most necessary.

Peace Time Preparations—Preparedness.—During peace time, weapons, clothing and equipment are naturally arranged in a prescribed place in barracks. Each article should be so arranged that the soldier will put his hand on it naturally, even in the darkness, or in emergencies. On account of the articles being in a fixed place, the soldier often does not realize the advantage of being able to grasp them readily. If the difficulty of searching for obscure articles in the dark be considered, one must realize the great advantage of being able to reach them naturally and easily. Accordingly, while resting on the march, in camp, billet, or bivouac, articles will always be arranged in an orderly manner, so that they may be seized quickly and certainly.

IV.

TRAINING IN DRESSING.

Occasions.—This training should be carried out at the same time as the ordinary day training. There are two opportunities for this:

1. At the time of changing the daytime course of training.

2. It can be carried out especially as a drill in dressing.

In the first instance, have the men dress in a fixed place, with each article in a special place. It is important to employ the time so as not to enroach upon time allotted to other drills.

Orderly Methods.—In the second instance, the following points are important:

1. A comprehension of the method of dressing. While explaining this in barracks, or in a fixed position, give a signal by a whistle, and say: "Now put on such and such a thing." While assistants instruct and inspect the men, teach them the basic principles of what they are doing.

2. Make them dress, unexpectedly, in daytime.

3. Explain the method of dressing at night.

4. Make them dress, unexpectedly, at night.

By such a method of training, the objective may be attained. At this time, without fail, coolness, order and quiet must be maintained. At first, pay no attention to the time consumed; after a little while, demand more speed, and finally have the movement executed at the rate desired.

Number of Times Practiced.—Whenever an army is accustomed to a certain manner of dressing in its daily life, the dressing is not a difficult matter. On that account, time is not specially allotted for such training, but practice will be had whenever there is a good opportunity. However, the following important principles must not be forgotten:

1. To guard against negligence.
2. To review the methods of dressing.

For this reason, it should be practiced every month or so, and whenever the men become careless about it.

V.

NIGHT AND VISION.

Importance of Cultivating the Vision at Night.—At night, one is able to see according to the degree of darkness. The amount of vision also differs naturally and it is important to know the amount under various circumstances. Especially is this true under circumstances where the judgment cannot be formed by hearing, *i. e.*, in rainy weather, or under other noisy conditions, where vision, though insufficient, is superior to hearing. Therefore, the training of the eye at night is a most important matter, as, to a certain degree, it can be strengthened by experience and practice. In the Japanese-Russian War, the judgment by sight of soldiers accustomed to the terrain and to night movements, was surprisingly good, and was entirely due to experience.

Vision at Night Can Be Improved by Training.—One accustomed to night movements, compared to one not so accustomed, is much more able to form correct judgments by sight; for experience sharpens the nerves and increases the faculty of attention. From indications, from methods of comparison, together with other assisting factors, one's judgment soon becomes accurate.

Night Vision—Detecting and Losing Sight of.—Vision at night differs in degree, also, according to the concentration of attention; in this connection, the following principles are from my own experience:

1. When you follow with your eyes a thing once discovered, you will be able to see it for a long distance.

2. The distance at which you first discover an object, is less than the distance where you loose sight of it. Therefore, at night, when you lose sight of an object you have once discovered, it is difficult to find it a second time. When you follow it with your eye vision is easy, and the distance at which the object is visible becomes much greater, especially if there are supplementary indications. In such a case a thing liable to be unnoticed, will be seen by the observer.

Night Vision and Objects, and the Color of Surrounding Objects.—The color of the dress has great bearing on vision; and I have learned the following facts from my own observation:

1. On a·dark night a white coat can be seen farther than a black one.

2. When there is moonlight, often a black coat can be seen farther than a white one.

3. In any case, a light brown or mouse color can be seen a long distance.

4. A black color against a black background is more difficult to see than white; the latter against white surroundings is more difficult than black.

From these facts, the importance of bearing in mind the color of surrounding objects when fixing the kind of dress, or determining one's movements, is apparent.

Night Vision and Relations of Light and Shadow.—
Night vision differs greatly according to one's position
relative to a luminous body and shadow:

1. When a luminous body, such as the moon, is
faced, vision is decreased.

2. When the light is behind, vision is increased.

3. When a luminous body is overhead, the mean
of increase and decrease is the same.

4. Even though facing the light, if it does not
strike the eyes directly, it injures vision but little.

5. One can see when looking from darkness into
light, but not when looking from light into darkness.

6. While holding the light yourself, only your own
surroundings can be seen.

7. When a light is behind an object, the latter's
outlines are clearly visible.

8. A black object or a moving object covered by
shadow, is difficult to see.

9. Small objects seem far away, and large ones
seem near.

10. Bright objects appear near, and obscure ones,
far away.

The above facts teach one that, when covered by
dark objects, or when moving in the shadow, to look
at the bright side from the dark as much as possible,
and not have the light directly in front.

Relation of the Seasons to Night Vision.—

1. In level, open country, the field of view is extensive.

2. In close country, the opposite is true.

Accordingly, from late in the autumn until the beginning of spring, on account of the grass having withered and the leaves fallen the field of view is extensive. From late in the spring until early autumn on account of the luxuriant grass and trees, the field of view is restricted. During the Manchurian winter (in level country), the field of view is greater than in Japan. In mountainous localities, trees are few, compared to Japan, and the field of view is correspondingly greater.

Night Vision and our own Posture.—In looking at objects which have ground objects in their rear, a standing posture is advisable; without such objects in rear, a low posture is best. Therefore, to avoid being seen, take a low posture; if moving, keep physical objects in your rear. Even though such objects be distant, they will be of great assistance.

Night Vision and Field Glasses.—Whenever there is light at night from moon or stars, and at twilight and dawn, field glasses will double the power of vision. However, as the glasses narrow the field of view, it is dangerous to depend upon them, except to confirm a thing already seen, or when the locality in which the object to be seen, will appear and move, is fixed.

VI.

METHOD OF TRAINING NIGHT VISION.

General Principles.—In this training, have the men learn thoroughly the preceding principles. After they have become somewhat experienced, teach them the subject of relative vision under all kinds of circumstances. This will give them a suitable standard of judgment; and it is most necessary that the soldier have various kinds of experiences, so that he may learn how to act when alone.

Important Points of Training.—

1. The execution of movements at night, without reference to the amount of light. In this case, the following training is suggested for the vision:

(*a*) A single soldier moving quietly, first toward the soldier under instruction, and second away trom him. The reason for the quiet movement is to prevent any assistance from sound, thus training the soldier in relative vision.

(*b*) A single moving soldier allowing some noise, such as the noise of the bayonet scabbard, water in the canteen, footsteps, etc., first toward the man under instruction, and second away from him.

(*c*) A single soldier in different colored clothing, both toward and away from the man under instruction.

(*d*) After a little while, increase the number of soldiers and have them move under the following conditions: 1. Quietly; 2. Under ordinary conditions; 3. With different colored clothing; Toward the one under instruction (discovery), and away from him (losing sight of).

(*e*) With a squad under the same conditions as paragraph (d).

2. Taking the light into consideration.

(*a*) With the light (moon, lantern, etc.), above and in the rear.

(*b*) With the light at a high place in the front.

(*c*)   With the light in rear of the object to be seen.

(*d*)   When the object to be seen bears the light.

(*e*)   When the man under instruction bears the light.

(*f*)   When the object to be seen is on the sky-line, and when not.

(*g*)   Movements in the shadow.

(*h*)   The relation between one hidden by an object and one covered by a shadow.

The above practice should be carried out, first, quietly; second, **under** ordinary conditions; third, with different colored uniforms.

Methods of Training.—When the number of soldiers under instruction is small, one instructor supervises the instruction in one squad; if the number be large, there will be assistant instructors in charge of each squad. The instruction of all squads will be carried out at the same time, taking care that they be so placed so as not to interfere with each other.

♭ *B*

R

Squad.

For example, place a squad at A. From this squad send one man (later several men) in the direction B. When he is about to disappear from view, halt him and estimate the distance. Again, based on these principles, send one man (later, several) outside the field of view, in the direction B. with instructions to advance toward A. When he enters the field of view, halt him and estimate the distance.

Try these experiments just mentioned in the following cases and make each man judge distance, etc., for himself, first, quietly; second, under ordinary conditions (singly, several men, squad); third, with different colored uniforms.

Experiments.—When this kind of training is finished cultivate the understanding and power of judgment by movements at will over various kinds of terrain and under varying conditions of weather, darkness, etc. Teach them to utilize trees, light, terrain, etc., the instructors correcting and criticising the movements. For example, form the men into a squad, and have other soldiers, from a considerable distance outside the limit of vision, move toward the squad, making use of light, terrain, shadows, etc., as already explained. The squad will watch and criticise the movements, the instructor also adding his criticism. Suitable occasions for teaching the relations of terrain, natural objects, weather, luminous bodies, etc.

VII.

HEARING AT NIGHT.

At night, on account of the difficulty of vision, the ears must be trained to listen attentively, and with judgment; the military objective must be attained by a combination of sight and hearing. Even when you cannot approach an 'object close enough to see it. In many cases, the terrain and the state of the enemy will enable you to accomplish your object by hearing. Again, in many cases, hearing enables one to judge of the proximity of the enemy, and of his movements. Therefore the scope of practical use of hearing at night is very extensive; and it is important that the hearing be well trained so that one may be able to guess all indications coming from sounds, and at the same time so plan his own movements so as not to furnish the enemy with such indications. On that account, it is necessary to have a criterion by which indications may be judged, and a self-consciousness by which one can regulate his own movements.

The Character of the Ground and Sounds.—

1.   If the ground be hard, the echo is loud.

2.   If the ground be soft, there is but little echo.

That is, if the ground be hard, the noise is sharp; if soft, it is dull.

Kinds of Covering Substances and Sound.—Noise varies according to the kind of covering substance; therefore it is very necessary to know the relative amount of sound when walking over various kinds of ground.

The Size of a Detachment and the Relative Weight of Materials.—If a detachment be large, it causes a corresponding amount of noise; and can be heard at a distance; if it be small, the noise is small. If the materials be heavy, the noise carries a great distance, and if they be light, the contrary is true. These relations are coexistent with those of the character of the ground.

Weather.—

1. Rain and snow.

(*a*) When rain is falling there are great differences in hearing, depending upon the degree of rain.

(*b*) When snow is falling, the amount of obstruction to noise, compared to rain, is small. When passing over snow, it varies according to the degree of freezing.

2. *Wind.*—

(*a*) When there is no wind, conditions are excellent for hearing, as sound is not at all obstructed.

(*b*) When the wind is blowing, conditions are favorable for hearing sounds which occur in the direction from which the wind is blowing, and noises can be heard at a long distance. Opposite conditions produce exactly opposite results.

(*c*) Wind blowing in one's ears is disadvantageous, as the noise interferes with hearing.

3. Time of night.

At dead of night, surrounding noises can be heard better than at twilight or dawn.

4. Relation of physical objects.

In level open country, which has no trees, buildings, etc., to interfere with the transmission of sound, noises travel far.

5. Relation of seasons.

In the winter, not only is the ground frozen, but the leaves of plants, trees, etc., are fallen, the grass is withered and dead, and the crops cut and gathered; therefore, sounds travel especially far.

VIII.

TRAINING IN HEARING AT NIGHT.

Important Points to be Considered.—In the following training, have the men understand clearly the relations of the manner of walking, numbers and clothing, to the sound produced; then extend the training as follows:

1. The march of infantry.

(*a*) A quiet advance.

(*b*) Quick time not in steps (single soldier, several men, squad with and without arms, in different kinds of weather and over different kinds of ground).

(*c*) Quick time in step, under same conditions as (b).

(*d*) Double time.

2. March of cavalry.

This should be carried out whenever there is a good opportunity, conformable to the above principles.

3. March of artillery.

To be carried out as in (1).

4.   The noise of intrenching.

(*a*)   The noise of digging with a pick.

(*b*)   The noise of driving a shovel strongly into the ground.

(*c*)   The noise of pushing a spade into various kinds of ground.

(*d*)   The noise of a squad carrying on the work freely.

Methods.—The apportionment of squads according to the number of men, is the same as previously described.

For example, have the necessary number of men advance from the squad at A, in the direction of B. Having faced the squad at A to the rear, have them listen to the noise of intrenching at B; when they can no longer hear it, halt the squad at B, and estimate the distance. Again, have a squad at B, approach the squad at A; when the latter can hear the noise, have them estimate the distance. This training should be carried out with a varying number of men, and under varying conditions of ground and weather. By such means, each man, individually, will learn the proper pace and manner of advance; the noise of working, also, will teach them how to use their tools with a minimum of noise. The following exercises, also, are important: The intrenching of a squad (of so many men) at what distance can it be heard, (a) in quiet weather, (b) when the wind is favorable, (c) when wind is unfavorable, etc.

Inferences to be drawn from Sound.—To state it briefly, one who is accustomed to noticing sounds at night, is able to form his judgment of the causes by using the various inferences that may be drawn from such sounds. For this reason, such basic instruction is very necessary for soldiers; this instruction, also, will give them a basis for the guidance of their own movements. For this purpose, it is important to take advantage of every opportunity for instruction in comparing the causes which give rise to the sounds, to the sounds themselves, as for example, the march of a detachment, cavalry, wagons, etc. When well trained in this, the soldier will be able to guess the direction of march, the approximate position with reference to himself, distance, etc. If no good opportunities for such training present themselves, while moving on the many roads, or in their vicinity, listen to all the sounds which arise on the road and practice estimating their causes, direction, distance, etc.

It is very necessary to be able to judge by hearing, the noise of the enemy's artillery entering a position, and the intrenching of infantry. The Japanese-Russian War taught us the necessity of often changing our positions to conform to those of the enemy made during the night; and our only way of determining those movements was from the noise of batteries going into position, intrenching, etc.

IX.

QUIET MARCH AT NIGHT.

Importance.—A quiet march is not only important for the purpose of taking the enemy unawares, but, at the same time, it prevents confusion in our own ranks. A quiet night march demands absolute silence and a suitable pace. In the Japanese-Russian War, although it was difficult for large bodies to move without the noise of marching, the advantage of quiet movements was indisputably shown. There are many cases in which an absolutely quiet march is demanded of individuals, such as patrols, outposts, etc.; such training should be borne in mind when these men become units of a larger force.

Important Cautions in a Night March.—

1. Care as to clothing.

It is important that there be no noise from the clothing and equipments; this should be true at double time as well as at quick time. To carry this into effect, the following points must be especially borne in mind:

(*a*) That there shall be no noise from the ammunition in the ammunition boxes.

(*b*) That no noise arises from the movements of the bayonet scabbard.

(*c*) The belt must be kept tight without fail.

(*d*) That the contents of the haversack make no noise.

(*e*) When the overcoat is worn, the skirt must be fastened up.

2. Individual precautions.

(*a*)   When coughing cannot be prevented, cover the mouth with the coat sleeve.

(*b*)   Be careful to hold the rifle so that it will not strike the ground.

(*c*)   See that no noise arises from the rifle sling and swivel.

3. A detachment.

(*a*)   Each soldier will take care not to bump into his neighbor.

(*b*)   There will be no talking between adjacent files.

(*c*)   Each soldier will take care not to make it necessary to leave ranks (for lost clothing, equipment, etc.).

4. Manner of walking.

(*a*)   In short grass, raise the feet high.

(*b*)   In long grass, keep the feet low.

(*c*)   In climbing a hill, plant the toe first.

(*d*)   In descending a hill, plant the heel first.

(*e*)   Don't stumble or fall down.

5. Connection.

(*a*)   In-line, conform to the movements of the soldier on the right or left; in column, on the soldier in front.

(*b*)   Don't hang the head; if this is done, connection will surely be lost.

(*c*)   Don't leave ranks, or halt unnecessarily.

(*d*)   At a halt, close up, but do not bump against the man in front.

(*e*)   Listen to signals, commands, etc., and be sure not to mistake them.

X.

TRAINING IN QUIET MARCHES AT NIGHT.

Dress.—At first, the training should be without arms, proceeding step by step until fully armed and equipped. During this time, the men must study how to prevent any noise arising from any part of their dress or equipment.

Order of Training.—General explanations will be made to the men on the ground where the quiet night march is to be made. After indicating the manner of walking, each soldier will be made to practice it under the supervision of an officer, who will explain the principles involved. When these principles have been understood, the number of men will be gradually increased, and the principles of the quiet march, individually, and by squad, will be taught.

Method of Carrying Out the Above Training.—This training will be carried out at the same time and with the same formations as the training for hearing.

Cautions.—Although a quiet night march is very important, it must not be allowed to injure the offensive spirit. A quiet movement never means a spiritless one, and it must be made clearly evident that minute care never means hesitation. In a quiet night march all noise will be prohibited, and each man must take care not to cause confusion to the entire command by his individual mistakes and errors.

XI.

THE CROSSING OF ROUGH GROUND AT NIGHT.

Importance of Practice.—At night, the different ground objects differ in aspect from the daytime. Objects, which in the day are no great obstacle, become formidable at night. Open level country which can be easily crossed at night, cannot be expected in practice; accordingly, the crossing of rough ground, orderly, quickly and exactly, without confusion and without delay, is a very important thing for an army. If proper training be had, such a movement is not very difficult; training insures a minimum of fatigue and disorder.

Summary.—

1. As falling down often follows a stumble, care must be taken not to stumble. Even after stumbling, one is not liable to fall down unless leaning forward; therefore, that tendency must be avoided.

2. As falling down is sometimes unadvoidable, the following precautions must not be neglected:

(*a*) Arrange clothing, equipment, etc., so that there will be nothing lost or broken; special care must be taken not to lose the hat.

(*b*) Not to drop or break the rifle.

(*c*) Not to talk or make any noise.

3. The method of carrying the rifle varies with the ground and ground objects; in a forest, etc., it is a good thing to carry it in the hand, taking proper care not to cause any danger to the rank in front.

4. If, while in a squad, the soldier only pays attention to what is underneath his feet, the following disadvantages must occur:

(*a*) The march will be delayed.

(*b*) Collision in front and rear.

(*c*) Loss of connection.

5. When obstacles are encountered, they will be passed in accordance with the principles laid down under that subject.

XII.

TRAINING IN CROSSING ROUGH GROUND AT NIGHT.

Clothing.—In these movements, care in the matter of dress is especially important. If untrained men are made to carry arms from the very first, not only will the rifles get broken, but the men will sustain personal injuries as well. Therefore, if practicable, dummy guns should be substituted for the service rifles in the early stages of the training; this training should be carried out in the following order:

(*a*) Without arms.

(*b*) With dummy rifles.

(*c*) With service rifles.

(*d*) With full equipment.

Order of Training.—

1. At the very first, the training should be individual, allowing an abundance of time for the execution of the movement; at this time the principles should be thoroughly inculcated.

2. Proceed, in a short time, by squad; at first, from column of fours in single rank extending to double and quadruple ranks, and in line as well. At times, have a simple change of direction or formation executed. The change of direction by squad to the right or left is simple, and will be of practical use; it is important, also, to teach, practically, such important movements as the change of formation from column to line, line to column, company column to line, etc.

3. When well trained in these movements, require them to be made silently. Even though the passage of uneven ground is a difficult matter, repeated practice makes it comparatively easy. During the Japanese-Russian War, the greater part of those who fell down during such movements were newly arrived reservists.

XIII.

DETERMINATION OF DIRECTION AT NIGHT.

Its Importance.—That the determination of direction, day or night, is important, is clearly evident. Especially at night, it is easy to mistake directions, and it is difficult to discover the mistake quickly. If the direction is once mistaken, the execution of one's mission is practically impossible; therefore, the quick determination of direction, at any time, is a most important matter.

Methods of Determining Direction.—By fixed Stars:

1. Direction can be determined by the position of the greater number of fixed stars, especially by the north star. Accordingly, on a clear night, the direction can

be accurately fixed by this star. The north star is a fixed star in the tail of the Little Bear constellation. It is on the prolongation of the line b—a, which connects two stars of the Great Bear constellation, and at about

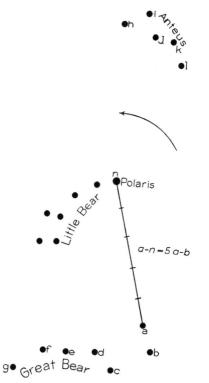

five times the distance between these two stars. On one flank of the Little Bear constellation, which is opposite the Great Bear, is a collection of stars in the shape of a cross, called Anteus.* Anteus always moves,

*The constellation shown in the cut and noted in the text as "Anteus" is the well known one of "Cassiopeia." It is in the form of an irregular letter "W" instead of being in the shape of a cross as stated above.—*Translator.*

maintaining this relation with the north star at the center. Therefore, when these stars are seen, the recognition of the north star is easy, and the north can be fixed.

2. Method by the moon.

Although it is difficult to determine direction by the position of the moon, the latter has the advantage of being recognizable even on nights when all the stars cannot be seen. The moon crosses the meridian about noon on the first lunar day, and it moves about fifty minutes behind the sun every day. Therefore, if the age of the moon be known, the approximate passing of the meridian can be easily computed. Its approximate age can be computed from the shape of its bright portion.

3. Method by a map.

A map indicates directions in a general way, by its outlines. Either the uppper portion is north, or the direction is indicated. Therefore, if the map can be oriented upon the actual ground, direction can be easily determined. Even though such an orientation is difficult at night, the general directions can be fixed from memory, or from the direction of roads, mountains or rivers. If there be a compass it can be done simply and conveniently.

4. Method by compass.

The blue end of the needle generally indicates the north. In a dense fog, snow storm, or in the darkness within a forest, in all cases when a mark is difficult to see, there is no way as certain as the compass.

5. Other methods.

The condition of trees, the position of the windows in houses in cold countries, the direction of prevailing winds of a locality, the position of wind shelters, wind mills, etc., all aid in determining direction.

XIV.

TRAINING IN DETERMINING DIRECTION.

How to Find the North Star and How to Use it.— In locating the north star, the instructor first points it out to each soldier. Next, he explains its relations to the previously described constellations. At another time, he will take the same men away from barracks, and have them individually, locate the star. Practice will soon enable them to look up and discover it quickly. When once discovered, it fixes the north, and the other directions easily follow. Next, using this star as a guide, order the men to move in any required direction, by such commands, as: "Move southeast; northwest; etc." When they can do this accurately, they have learned how to use the star.

Method by Looking at the Compass.—When examining a compass, except on a moonlight night, a light must be made, and each soldier requires practice on that point.

XV.

METHOD OF MAKING A LIGHT AT NIGHT.

Its Importance.—In any case, it is important that the light should not be visible to the enemy, either directly or from its reflection on trees, etc.; therefore, the following principles must be observed:

(a)   That the light does not leak out directly.

(b)   That it is not reflected by any object.

Manner of Making a Light.—From the preceding principles, we see that the proper way to make a light, is to take advantage of the configuration of the ground, the various pyhsical objects, etc.   The following are examples:

1.   If there are any trees in the vicinity, make the light behind them using the body also to shelter it.

2.   Use embankments, houses, stone walls, etc., in the same way.

3.   When there are no such covering objects, proceed as follows:

(a)   Two men clasp arms together, their backs toward the enemy; using their bodies as a shelther, hold the cap near the ground, and make a light in the cap.

(b)   Use the cape of the overcoat as a shelter for the light.

(c)   One man alone, will squat down on the ground, and make a light between his legs, the ground, and the upper part of his body.

(*d*) Light the tobacco (Japanese), in the pipe quickly; blow it, and examine the object (watch compass, etc.).

Individual Training.—After the above basic methods are understood, each man will be made to carry matches, and lights will be made singly or in groups, and then inspected. For example, have the men under instruction advance the necessary distance in front of the squad A; at that place, have them make a light so that it will not be visible from A. If a light be seen, have the one who made it do it over and instruct him carefully.

This Method is a Common Sense One.—As this method is a common sense one, much instruction will not be necessary. It will be sufficient, to test the memory at times. Thoughtful soldiers will do this, properly, even without instruction.

XVI.

CONNECTION AND CONNECTING FILES AT NIGHT.

Methods.—

1. Method by sound.

On a dark night, a luminous medium is necessary in maintaining connection by sight. Accordingly, when conditions forbid the use of a light, sound must be depended upon and preconcerted signals are required. For example:

(a) Sound made by striking the rifle butt.

(b) Use of the whistle.

(c) In addition, various methods suitable to the conditions.

When such signals become complicated, their usefulness is destroyed; they must therefore, be very simple. For example:

(a) Signal for attention.

(b) Signal for announcing one's position.

(c) Signal when the enemy, or something suspicious is discovered.

(d) Signals for advance, retreat, summoning, etc.

These signals may be fixed by the tone of the whistle, or by the number of blows struck on the rifle butt. In this instruction, have the assistant instructors, at first, give these signals to the recruits; and then have the signals agreed upon carried out within the squad of recruits under the supervision of the instructors.

2. Method of connection by signals.

Methods of communication on a large scale by revolving or flashing lights, etc., are very important, but we shall only discuss the simpler methods here.

(a) Beacon lights.

(b) Matches.

(c) Match-cord.

(d) Bull's-eye lantern.

(e) White cloth.

During the Japanese-Russian War, beacon lights were frequently used, especially by the Russians.

Lanterns, straw, or some combustible material was tied on the end of poles, which were erected at necessary places (oil was used if there was any on hand). On account of the nature of the work, it was usually performed by officers, as it was found dangerous to entrust it to enlisted men.

Matches cannot be used for connection, except in the very simplest cases. For example, they can only be used for the advance or retreat of patrols, or for the transmission of very important single signals.

By a rope match, comparatively many signals can be transmitted, as for example:

(a) The round one has a certain meaning.

(b) The flat one has a certain meaning.

(c) The vertical one has a certain meaning.

In addition, by various complicated vibrations, many different signals can be transmitted. The distances at which this rope match is visible are fixed by experiments, and each soldier must be taught the effective distance.

Dark lanterns can be used at short distances in flashing messages. Though the distance of transmission varies with the strength of the flame, it can, under many conditions, reach a comparatively great distance. When accustomed to this method of transmission, it will be found very convenient for outpost duty, and it has the further advantage of being concealed from the enemy. During the Japanese-Russian War, the author made one out of an empty vegetable can. Each squad was supplied with one of these cans, and they proved of great value.

3. Connecting files.

Even though the movement of connecting files at night are similar to those in the day time, the amount of difficulty varies greatly. Accordingly, training under varying conditions is necessary. The terrain, state of the roads, conditions of the hour, etc., have a great influence. This work must be carried out accurately in the following directions:

(a) In a longitudinal direction, at a halt and when connecting moving bodies.

(b) In a horizontal direction under similar conditions.

4. Messengers.

The proper performance of the duties of night messengers is very difficult, because at night time, on account of losing directions, mistaking roads, together with the mental state of doubt and fear of the messenger, there are many times when their movement is stopped, or their objective not carried out. The progress in the use of the telephone, telegraph, and other methods of transmission, has not rendered the training of messengers useless.

5. Methods by which messengers may advance.

(a) By roads.

(b) By rushes, from object to object.

(c) Moving along a prominent extended physical object (as river, mountain, forest, etc.).

(d) In a certain fixed direction (by compass, etc.).

(e) By a mark, light, etc.,

The method by roads is very safe if the roads are prominent, and there is no danger of losing the way. Such roads as those of China which connect village with village, are very uncertain and it was very easy to get lost. When travelling on a road, the following precautions are important:

1. Care and discrimination in the forks of a road.

2. Marks or signs at important places.

3. Pay attention to physical objects on the road, or at the side of the road.

4. Other unusual relations.

5. The relation between the gradual change in the direction of a road and the forks of a road.

6. The manner in which a road enters or leaves a village.

For example, in sending an orderly from B to A, give him directions about the road he is to follow, in this manner: "Move from B toward A; at the three forks in the road near an umbrella-shaped pine tree, take the right road; after crossing a bridge, you will hear the noise of a water-wheel; continuing on this road, you will see a village on the left, which you will be able to pick out from its fire-tower, and A is but about five minutes walk beyond, etc." (See sketch p. 50).

The method of advancing by rushes from object to object, was used in crossing the Manchurian rice fields in winter, and in crossing ground where there were no roads. Such conditions forced us to adopt the above method.

7. Cautions respecting the above method:

(a) After entering the physical object (woods, etc.), do not mistake the direction on exit.

(b) If possible to pass around the flank of the object, it is preferable to going through it.

(c) The interior of villages and woods are important, but it is best not to enter them, except when clearly advantageous to do so; roads in the interior of a village are complicated, and it is often easy to lose

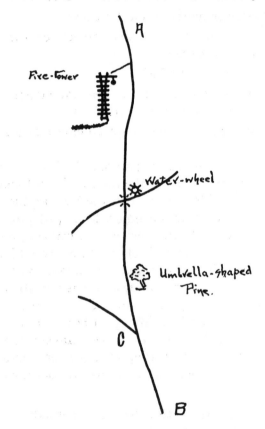

direction. When there is no map, memorize beforehand the names of the villages in order, as it will facilitate communication with the inhabitants of those villages. When advancing in an unknown country, you will be able to take proper road to the next village even though the natives could not tell you the road to the destination of the day's march. Whenever there are no natives, or you cannot communcicate with them, it is difficult to advance without a map. In such cases, objects or marks previously noted in the daytime must be depended upon, but it is a most difficult matter, at best.

8. Method by moving along a prominent extended object (river, woods, etc.).

For example, in going from A to B, when the road is indistinct and cannot be used, follow along the stream which flows in the direction A—B. In important cases, the messenger will go down to the stream to verify the road. (See sketch p. 52).

By this method, or by the direction of mountain ranges, rice-fields, ravines, etc., the general direction can be kept, but great obstacles will frequently be encountered, which only determination and boldness will conquer.

9. A messenger's looking forward and backward, and memory.

A messenger must always pay attention to the following things with reference to the road traversed, or physical objects passed on the way:

(a) Look back at the physical objects which he passes and at other things which will serve as marks, committing them all to memory.

(b) Memorize physical objects which are at important points (so that he will be able to recognize those points upon arrival there).

(*c*) In the daytime, think of the night; memorize **the marks**, and at the same time, judge how the shadows **will** appear at night. (Remember that projecting

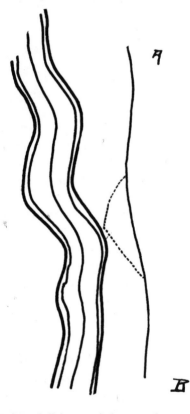

trees will not be visible at night, as they will be covered by objects in rear.).

(*d*) Establish special recognizing marks, as:

1. White cloth, white paper, etc., in branches of **trees.**

2. Special guiding trees.

3. Scatter paper, white powder, or other easily recognizable substances along the road.

Cautions for all Connecting Files.—

(*a*) Avoid the double time for connecting purposes. It is not only noisy, but there is the danger of falling down as well.

(*b*) The amount of sound required when reporting and for connection purposes will vary according to the conditions which obtain at the time.

(*c*) Connecting files of a column, upon arriving at a fork in the road, must not lose touch with the column in rear or lose sight of the detachment in front. At such times, paper or white powder will be scattered (See chapter relating to night marches).

(*d*) The position of connecting files should be such that they can see our own forces, and be seen by them.

(*e*) They must make the transmission of messages quick and certain.

10. Method by relays.

(*a*) Long distance relays—written and verbal messages.

(*b*) Short relays—written and verbal messages.

The method by relays is frequently carried out in war time, and it is therefore necessary that all soldiers be well trained in this work. In the training for long distance relays, it is very important to begin with very simple methods, gradually working up to difficult conditions.

For example, place soldiers as indicated above; from the position of the instructor at A, give verbal orders and messages to No. 1 in the vicinity of the instructor, and cause the message to be transmitted to Nos. 2, 3, etc., to the last post, who transmits it to the instructor. This exercise can be carried out during other drills, or while on the march.

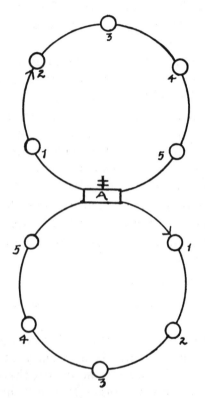

In short relays, also, it will be found profitable to begin the training as described above. Whenever necessary, the message will be transmitted in a low tone from one soldier to another. Practice may be carried out during night maneuvers, or on the march.

XVII.

NIGHT FIRING.

Night firing must not be carried out unnecessarily; however, if conditions are such that it can be carried out accurately and without danger, it is permissible. Night firing by squad is most effective in volley firing by command; but it is important that training in individual fire, also, be carried out, as that kind of firing must be used at point blank ranges.

Cautions for Individuals when Firing.—

1. At night, keep cool and obey the commands of your leader.

2. Night firing is usually too high; therefore, take care not to incline the upper part of the body to the rear, or raise the muzzle of the rifle above the horizontal.

3. In firing at night, it is a good thing to release the trigger by one pressure of the finger, instead of the usual method.

4. Never get excited after firing; keep cool.

5. When firing is stopped, turn the safety without fail.

XVIII.

TRAINING IN NIGHT FIRING.

Horizontal Firing and Posture.—The kneeling position is most suitable for horizontal firing; when aiming, raise the buttock from the right heel and hold the rifle as in the standing position. This method of aiming is suitable to all kinds of terrain, and can be done in double rank as well as in single rank.

Method and Order of Training.—This training may carried out as follows:

(*a*)   Train each soldier to hold his rifle horizontally.

(*b*)   By such training he will soon be able to hold it so, naturally.

1.   Formation.

The following points are essential:

(*a*)   One soldier must not interfere with another.

(*b*)   It must be convenient for supervision by an officer.

In line with one pace interval fulfills both these requirements.   This drill trains the muscles to work involuntarily; and daytime will be found most convenient for training and supervision.

2.   Opportunity for training.

Daytime is best for this training, on account of its convenience for observation and instruction.

3.   Methods.

Have each soldier close his eyes and level his rifle, according to the principles that have been explained to him.   After the rifle has been brought against the cheek, the soldier will open his eyes and examine it.   Next have this movement executed by squad by command, just as in pointing and aiming drill.   When this movement is well understood, order the men to close their eyes, and, while in that condition, put up a target and have them carry out horizontal fire against it.

XIX.

NIGHT BAYONET EXERCISES.

Importance of Such Drill.—A night battle is a hand to hand fight in which the bayonet must be used; therefore, the bayonet is the one cause of success in night attacks. When well trained in such fighting, it raises self-confidence, increases bravery, and drives away fear.

Cautions in the Use of the Bayonet at Night.—

1. At night, on account of an excessive watchfulness, there is a tendency to misjudge the proximity of the enemy, and to dash upon him with the determination to overthrow him with the body alone, without making use of the bayonet.

2. Make the men understand that they can overthrow the enemy only after they have first put away all thought of their own lives.

3. At the time of the attack and charge, it is important not to stumble and fall; in order to avoid this, care must be exercised in placing the feet on the ground.

4. Care will be exercised in the dress, and in the handling of dummy guns, etc.

5. An accurate and rigid posture is necessary in executing this movement in the prescribed namner.

6. During training, the following points will be observed:

(a) Be cool, and do not make any sound without permission.

(*b*)   High morale and overflowing spirits are necessary.

(*c*)   Cultivate an aggressive spirit.

XX.

TRAINING IN NIGHT BAYONET FENCING.

Scope of Training.—In night training in bayonet fencing, it will not be necessary to carry out all the movements given in the Fencing Manual, because at nighttime, it is important to overthrow the enemy in the first charge by a vigorous and violent offensive, in which skillful dexterity is no great necessity.   Therefore, the following training will be found sufficient:

(*a*)   Direct thrust against temporary targets.

(*b*)   Fundamental drill.

When these two things are taught sufficiently, the requirements of a night bayonet attack can be fulfilled.

Method of Training.—

1.   Against dummy figures.

Each soldier will be made to charge against a hypothetical enemy (as used in Russia), or against a white cloth, or figure of a man carried by the instructor.   At first the figure will be in a fixed position, but later, the soldier will charge seeking the target and not knowing its position beforehand.   As the training progresses, make surprise targtes of white cloth, dummy figures, targets, etc., and at suitable times, have them appear suddenly before the soldier.

2.   Fundamental training.

In this training, the instructor—Non-commissioned officer, or First Class Private—wears defensive armor, and if necessary, face armor as well. The soldiers under instruction wear fencing gloves only, or the regulation clothing. The instructor calls out a name, and the soldier charges several times, being relieved in turn. At this time the soldier must be taught not to fear the instructor's bayonet, but he must be made to approach very close to the instructor. Try to make the exercise as realistic as possible. On moonlight nights, this exercise will conform to that of the daytime, but the best way to take advantage of the light can be studied.

XXI.

NIGHT INTRENCHING.

Importance.—The construction of fortifications, on the offensive or defensive, in the day or night, is a most important matter. Even though prevented in daytime by the pressure of battle, the night will bring an opportunity for intrenching. Accordinlgy it follows, that, in many cases in actual warfare, intrenchments are constructed in front of the enemy at night. For this reason training in night intrenching is most necessary. While such work is comparatively easy on a moonlight night, it is a very difficult thing on a dark night.

Night Intrenching and Important Point in Training.—

1. Each man marks out his own section, and begins digging from close by his feet.

2. Care will be taken to connect the individual excavations.

3. It is easy to make the trench to narrow; therefore caution is enjoined in this respect.

4. Be careful that the excavated earth is not thrown too far or too near; each man will watch the way he throws the dirt and apply his strength accordingly.

5. In using the shovel and the spade, much noise is caused if the dirt be allowed to fall from an unnecessary height; therefore the strength should be applied when the shovel is near the ground.

6. Each man's section should be large enough to prevent his being struck by his neighbor's tools.

7. If discovered by the enemy's search lights, do not become confused; simply lie down.

8. If attacked by the enemy, do not throw the tools away; either put them in the place where the rifles were left, or in some other fixed position.

9. Do not use the pick unless necesssary, as this tool requires a wide frontage.

10. Do not scrape tools together in order to clean off the dirt; use a chip of wood or the toe of the shoe.

11. Cautions regarding reliefs:

(*a*) At the time of relief, intrenching tools will be handed to the relief without any talking.

(*b*) Care will be taken that no vacant spaces are left between the workmen.

(*c*) The working place should not be left, except upon arrival of the relief. Each man will carry his rifle.

(*d*) Whenever unadvoidable, leave the tools sticking up in the ground where they can be easily found.

In order to prevent losing them, it is a good thing to tie a piece of cloth on the handle.

XXII.

TRAINING IN NIGHT INTRENCHING.

Methods.—To carry out this training, march the squad on a dark night, to the training ground. First, have the men dig individually, and explain to them how it differs from the work in the daytime. Next, place two or more men side by side, indicate each one's sector, and have each one execute his prescribed portion. If possible to do so, it will be found advantageous for the men to see, in the day, the result of their night labors. At this time, too, they must be taught the differences in sound resulting from the differences in the character of ground and the tools used.

Cautions.—In this training, the following points should be especially noted:

1. At nighttime, do not have idle soldiers looking on at the work.

2. Take only a small squad at a time, as it is impossible to oversee, properly, the work of a large number.

3. In addition to their own work, have the men listen to the noise of others working, thus cultivating their judgment as to distance, number of men working, etc.

4. Don't limit the work to nighttime only. Make the men understand what is required by work in rainy and snowy weather, when such work is difficult.

5. Carry out this work as often as possible, so that they will become accustomed to it.

Method by Using Sand Bags.—(See detachment intrenching).

XXIII.

METHODS OF RECOGNIZING FRIENDLY TROOPS AT NIGHT.

Importance.—At night time there is danger of attacking and fighting our own forces; accordingly the quick recognition of our own troops is most important. If that recognition be delayed, there will be the great danger of losing the initiative.

Methods of Recognition.—

1. Speech.

(*a*) Different words from those in daily use.

(*b*) Countersign.

2. Uniform.

(*a*) Different from that in daily use.

(*b*) Special distinguishing marks.

Words and clothing in daily use are not sufficient to rely upon in war time. During the Japanese-Russian War, the Russians frequently wore our uniform, or Chinese clothing, and used our speech.

Disadvantages of Speech.—At night, the one who speaks first, is at a disadvantage. In the old days of sword and spear fighting, there was no particular danger in speech, unless very close together; but today, one who is believed to be an enemy, is quickly killed by firearms.

Suitable Methods of Recognition.—As stated above when there is a difference of language and uniform, that is a suitable method for quick recognition; but it is most important to gain the initiative. In order to prevent the enemy from gaining the initiative, such methods as striking the rifle stock, signals by whistle, etc., may be used, these methods being applicable to any country. However, on a very dark night, especially in a confused bayonet fight, such methods are not sufficient; accordingly, the men must wear some special distinguishing mark, which can be readily identified. In this case the distinguishing marks must be recognizable along the whole front, and, if possible, should be worn so as not to be visible to the enemy.

XXIV.

NIGHT DEMOLITION WORK.

Training.—When a position for assaulting is taken, the position of the enemy must be reconnoitered. Having made certain of the presence of obstacles in front of the enemy and their position and character, they must be destroyed before the charge. Engineer troops are most suitable for this work, but infantry, as well, must be able to open their own road. This demolition is a very difficult matter, especially in the case of independent infantry, not supplied with explosives. Therefore thorough training in peace time is most necessary.

Requisites for Demolition Work.—

(a) Brave men who do not fear death.

(b) Quick, clever men.

(c) Cool men.

Even though possessed of the above characteristics, if they do not take advantage of a good opportunity, success is uncertain. It is the duty of officers to watch for good opportunities.

Important Principles of Demolition Work.—Of course the point to be demolished must conform to the tactical requirements, and must be such a place that, having been broken, troops can enter instantly. The space demolished should be wide enough for a column of fours to pass through. Sufficient preparation should be made for this demolition, and its execution must be rapid. The obstacle should be approached, as far as possible, without the knowledge of the enemy; when this is impossible, it must be demolished under the protection of friendly troops. Several places should be selected for demolition so that there will be a good prospect of success somewhere.

Methods of Training.—This work is engineering work, and the men should be trained in it first in the daytime. After they thoroughly understand its requirements, the work will be carried on at night. While of course it is desirable that all men should have this training, on account of its difficult nature, it will be found sufficient to train only a selected number.

XXV.

METHODS OF USING HAND GRENADES AT NIGHT.

Hand grenades have become more important than ever on account of their practical use in the Japanese-Russian War; in future wars, their use will become more and more general. Even though there will be but few instances where great training will be required in their use, if they are not used properly success is impossible and they will only serve to alarm the enemy. Therefore each soldier will be trained in their use, at least to the extent of becoming brave enough to carry them without hesitation. On account of their danger, soldiers will first be accustomed to them in the daytime; then later, at nighttime, they will throw them at targets made of lanterns or lights. Whenever there are but few hand grenades, small packages of the same weight will be constructed; to these will be attached the same weight of throwing rope, and thus the effort necessary for throwing the grenades can be ascertained. Soldiers will thus learn the amount of effort necessary for various distances. The hurling of hand grenades is the prelude of the charge; if the charge comes too long after the shock of the grenades, success is most uncertain; the enemy's works must be penetrated immediately after the hand grenades are thrown.

XXVI.

NIGHT SENTINELS.

Training.—Sentinels will be trained in the daytime as well as at night. At night, he must be able to move under any condition that may arise during that time. This training should be begun only after the soldier understands clearly the essential points of the relations between sound and vision, the determination of direction, silent night marches etc.

Night, and Position of Sentinels.—(See chapter on sight and hearing).

1. A position with a broad field of view.

2. A position with no obstruction to the field of view.

3. A position where hearing is not interfered with.

4. A position not visible to the enemy, but convenient for our own view. For example:

(a) To keep open ground in front.

(b) To avoid a windy locality, or one where there are water-wheels, etc.

(c) At night, to be in the shadow of a tree with the moonlight behind.

(d) A position from which the sky-line is visible is advantageous, even on a dark night.

(e) A position where you can be seen a long distance against the sky-line, is disadvantageous.

(f) A position which is known to the natives is disadvantageous.

(g) To be always in a fixed position is disadvantageous.

(h) Terrain which prevents the enemy from attacking suddenly is advantageous.

Along the Shaho river in Manchuria, a sentinel in a fixed position was frequently surprised by the enemy, and there were many instances of such surprise caused by the fact that the natives knew the sentinel's position.

When in the daytime position at A, the sentinel can see well in the enemy's direction, but at night, such a position can be easily seen by the enemy; therefore the sentinel's post should be changed to B, from which place an enemy appearing at A can be easily discovered.

The sentinel's position should be chosen from the most suitable ones in the vicinity, and the sentinel, himself, should improve his post in accordance with previously mentioned requirements.

To stand carelessly with the rifle in the hand, naturally invites danger. This caution is especially important to men on such duties as sentinel on outpost, etc., which is the first line of defense of an army at the halt.

Night Sentinels and Posture.—The posture of sentinels will be laid down in instructions. In fixing the posture, the relation of the ground and physical objects must be borne in mind. At night, the following points will be especially noted:

(*a*) The posture should be lower than objects which are in rear.

(*b*) Avoid a posture visible on the sky-line.

(*c*) Other points are the same as in daytime.

Night Sentinels and Reconnaissance.—The principles of night reconnaissance depend upon the following points:

(*a*) Follow along physical objects as much as possible, keeping the body low, and holding the breath; you will thus be able to hear any noise.

(*b*) Try to see objects on the sky-line.

(c)   Bear in mind the relation between physical ob jects (trees, etc.) and the moon; take care that there is no enemy concealed in the shadow.

(d)   Form your judgement of conditions from the sounds heard.

(e)   Dont move unnecessarily.

A Sentinel's Challenge at Night.—Our preparation at night must be in accordance with the movements of the enemy.   Signals, countersigns, etc., will not be used unnecessarily.   It is important that we should know, first, something about the enemy.   At this time, the sentinel's posture will be in accordance with the following requirements:

(a)   When able to fire make preparations for so doing; if fired at by the enemy, take such a posture that you will not be hit, *i. e.*, lie down.

(b)   When there is no other course than the use of the bayonet, try to overthrow the enemy by one blow; care should be taken not to be surprised.

In short, challenge quickly, and do not allow the enemy to obtain the initiative.

Night Sentinels and Firing.—Sentinels should be careful about firing, even in the daytime; how much more is this true at night!   Such firing must conform to the following conditions:

(a)   When danger is pressing, and there is no time to return with a report.

(b)   Whenever necessary for the sentinel's own safety.

(c)   Whenever certain of hitting the enemy's patrols, etc.

(*d*) Whenever the enemy's returning patrol already knows the sentinel's position, and the latter is able to fire effectively.

We have already explained why sentinels should not fire unnecessarily at night. From experiences in actual warfare, it has been found that when a sentinel remains silent at his post, he gradually becomes excited, and fear and illusions fill his mind. Trees seem enemies, and naturally, firing soon follows.

During the Japanese-Russian War, when in contact with the enemy, the latter frequently attacked our sentinels in the following manner:

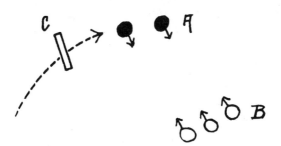

For example, some of the enemy's patrols about dusk, persistently operated in the direction B. Even at night they did not leave, but gradually approached closer in the drkness, just as if they were going to charge our post, and finallly opened fire. Our sentinels, being diverted by this, returned the fire. The enemy's detachment at C, locating the post by the flash and noise of firing, charged suddenly from C.

Sentinels confronting the enemy are in practically the same situation as in fortress warfare. Vigilance, of course, should be stricter than on the march; but there are many examples which show that the sentinel's firing guides the enemy and enables him to approach closely.

Night Sentinels and Reports.—Night sentinels, when making reports, will pay special attention to the following points:

(a) At the time of moving not to make any noise or cast any shadows.

(b) Not to move at the double time unless absolutely necessary, nor make any noise.

(c) The report will be made in a low voice, just mutually audible.

(d) At the time of the report (made to visiting patrols or others), not to let the enemy take advantage of it, or, if the enemy knows that one man has gone back to the rear to report, not to allow that fact to be taken advantage of.

(e) Not to mistake direction (when moving).

Night Sentinels and Connection.—A sentinel should be well acquainted with the neighboring posts, as there must be mutual connection in the line of sentinels. Therefore a sentinel should know the following things with reference to neighboring sentinels:

(a) The position and number of neighboring posts, both day and night.

(b) The shortest route to those posts.

(c) The difference in day and night methods of communication whether by movement or by sight.

(d) Movements and actions of a post when there is an emergency at a neighboring post.

A clear knowledge of conditions at neighboring posts is essential for the accurate execution of a post's own duties. During the Japanese-Russian War, many sentinels fell into the hands of the enemy while trying to connect with neighboring posts, not knowing that the latter had changed their positions. Again, often the enemy would appear in front of one post and open a violent fire, just as if they were about to attack it; while a hidden detachment attacked a neighboring post and took the sentinels prisoners. The following are the results of our experiences during the late war, concerning the communication of sentinels:

1. Visual signaling; observation.

Flags and other signals.

At night, lanterns. (When behind high ground, simple signals can be sent by disappearing lights).

2. Movements made by a moving sentinel.

(a) From one point to another.

(b) Advancing from both sides and meeting at a certain point.

(c) By a third person (visiting patrols, etc.).

During connection by a moving sentinel, there is a likelihood that the sentinel will be taken prisoner by the secret approach of the enemy, or that he will fall into some danger; therefore, sufficient quiet and caution are necessary.

Even though there is danger in always taking the same road, that danger must be disregarded if there is a good road within the line of sentinels. If the sentinel passes by way of the picket, quick communication can be made, but the space intervening cannot be patrolled while connection is being made.

Night Sentinels and Friendly Patrols.—When friendly patrols are about to cross the line of sentinels, the latter should be well trained in the proper procedure. The principal points are as follows:

(*a*) There must be a spirit of cooperation between patrol and sentinel.

(*b*) The sentinel must not be lazy or careless in his duties.

On this point, the following precautions are important:

(*a*) The sentinel will inform the patrol concerning what he has seen or heard about the enemy, and all things that the patrol ought to know.

(*b*) The sentinel must understand the configuration of ground, physical objects, and names of localities in front, so that he can explain them to the patrol.

(*c*) It is important that the sentinel know the patrol's duties, its road, objective of reconnaissance, the time and place of return, etc.

When a patrol is about to cross the line of sentinels and advance toward the enemy, the sentinel must not inform the patrol concerning the above mentioned points in a careless or perfunctory manner. The sentinel should regard the patrol as his partner, who is moving out to obtain information, and should do all in his power to assist the patrol in the proper performance of its duties. On this account, a sentinel, knowing that a patrol is out in front, will be able to judge the importance of rifle shots and other indications that he may hear. When the patrol returns to the line of sentinels, the latter will be informed concerning the following points:

(*a*) What the patrol has learned about the enemy.

(*b*) Whether or not any unusual signs were observed by the patrol, and, if so, what they were.

(*c*) Sentinels will question the patrol regarding designation of terrain, and any other points not clearly understood.

When a patrol leaves the line of sentinels, and advances to the front, neighboring sentinels will be notified by moving sentinels or other means.

A patrol is able to carry out its own duty well, by using what it has learned from the sentinel as a basis. That is why it is important that sentinels and patrols should work harmoniously together.

Night Sentinels and Reliefs.—Frequently the noise made by the relief, discovers the sentinel's position to the enemy, and this fact will be taken advantage of by a skillful enemy. Again, if the time of relief is known, the sentinel's position will be easily discovered.

Points which will be taught regarding reliefs:

(*a*) The amount of noise in transmitting general orders (if the sentinel knows them at the picket, or assembly place in rear, it is not necessary to repeat them every time).

(*b*) Cautions at time of transmission—matters relative to watchfulness, etc.

(*c*) Movements of new guard to sentinel's post.

(*d*) Their posture after arrival.

(*e*) Return of old guard and their subsequent movements.

At the time of transmission of orders, as few men as possible will appear at the post. Again, it will be found that some sentinels of the old guard will become inattentive, due to the relaxation of their previous mental strain—such men must be warned. New sentinels, also, on account of the presence of old sentinels at the time of relief, are liable to be neglectful in watching. On this account special care must be exercised, and training is important.

XXVII.

TRAINING OF NIGHT SENTINELS.

Training of Sentinels and Amount of Light.—The training of sentinels should be carried out at times in which the amount of light varies. That is, on moonlight, starry and dark nights, with and without wind, in rainy and snowy weather, etc.

Training of Sentinels and Terrain.—It is important that the training of night sentinels should be carried out in all kinds of terrain. In such varying terrain, the power of sight and hearing can be learned, both of which are most important for a sentinel to know.

Sentinels and Squads.—Although for the purpose of training, the number of men in a squad should be as few as possible, the time will be wasted if the incompetent Non-commissioned Officers and First Class Privates are placed in charge of the instruction. Trained men who understand thoroughly the ideas of the instructor, should be used for assistant instructors. Each assistant instructor will be shown the following:

(*a*) The squad's sector of ground, direction of operation, and kind of training to be carried out.

(*b*) Means and methods of training.

(*c*) Time to be employed for this purpose.

(*d*) Position and direction of indicated enemy.

(e) Signals for assembly, etc.

An Example of Such Training.—First have an old soldier or an assistant instructor execute the movement, while the men under instruction observe it (for this purpose a moonlight night, or just at dusk, is the best time); next, two or three men will carry out a similar movement, then proceed as follows:

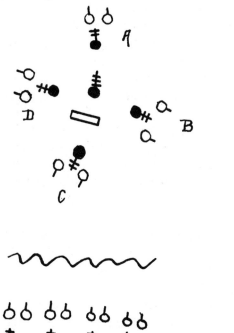

The instructor distributes the sentinels as in the upper sketch, and indicates the sector which they will watch. The remainder of the men are formed in a squad near the instructor and will form reliefs. An assistant instructor will be stationed in the vicinity of each sentinel. The instructor will direct his assistants to oversee the movements of the men while engaged on a certain duty, and to correct their mistakes. The necessary number of men will be sent out to represent the enemy; these men, having been given detailed instructions, will be guided by previously arranged signals (disappearing lights, bull's-eye lanterns, etc.). When all arrangements are completed, the instructor will direct the represented enemy to move, and the sentinels will oppose them. The instructor and his assistants criticise and instruct the men in their duties; or an assistant instructor will form a patrol of two or three men, and, when this patrol has arrived within the vicinity of a sentinel, will instruct the latter how to proceed. When these patrols have already gone out in front of the line of sentinels, they approach the sentinels as an indicated enemy. When the instruction on this point is finished, they change to friendly patrols, and instruct the sentinels upon that point.

Character of the Training.—The subjects in which the men will be trained do not differ from those in the daytime, *i. e.*, the principal points are as follows:

(*a*) Selection of sentinel's position.

(*b*) Sentinel's memory of physical objects.

(*c*) Sentinel's method of watching.

(*d*) Action with respect to patrols which cross line of sentinels.

(*e*)   Action to be taken with respect to indications heard.

(*f*)   Action with respect to the enemy.

(*g*)   Method of connection.

(*h*)   Method of reporting.

XXVIII.

NIGHT PATROLS.

Night Patrols and Methods of Connection.—Night patrols must be more careful than day patrols in keeping in touch; for in the daytime, even at long distances, connection can be maintained by sight, which, of course, is impossible at night. Special caution is required in the presence of the enemy, as it is then dangerous to use sound for the purpose of connection. Accordingly, the methods which can be used are as follows:

(*a*)   Diminish distances so that different subdivisions can see each other.

(*b*)   Use of the whistle.

(*c*)   Sounds made by striking the butt of the gun, or ammunition pouch.

The limit of communication by such methods is very restricted; therefore, it is often convenient that there be but one group executing a certain movement, but care must be taken that they are not all captured by the enemy at the same time.

Night Patrols and Methods of Maintaining Direction. —The difficulty of maintaining direction at night has already been mentioned; the patrol must strive by every means to maintain direction accurately. In order to do this, see those chapters where we have explained how to determine direction, and the chapter treating of the movements of connecting files.

Special cautions in various terrain are as follows:

1. Broad plains.

Movements in such a terrain must be in accordance with the following principles, as great errrors in direction arise from small differences in angles:

(a) Make reliable roads, or a prolonged physical object, the standard.

(b) Reliance on prominent objects.

(c) Reliance on the stars.

(d) Use of the compass.

(e) Use of maps.

(f) Reliance on the judgment of a well trained mind.

2. Woods.

It is as easy to mistake directions in woods as in open plains; often it will be so dark that no stars will be visible. The principles laid down under "Broad Plains," are equally applicable to "Woods."

3. Depressions.

After entering a depression, a mistake is often made in direction when going up again on high ground. The following precautions are therefore important.

(a) Before entering a depression, establish guiding points on high ground both front and rear.

(b) At the bottom of the depression, especially, make certain of the direction in which you will ascend.

(c) If necessary, establish other directions, also.

4. Obstacles.

When crossing obstacles, it is very easy to mistake directions even though advancing straight to the front. This is especially true when making a detour; the following cautions will be found important:

(a) Select guiding points in front and rear before crossing.

(b) Observe the direction of the obstacle, and calculate its angle with your previous road.

(c) If necesssary, determine the direction anew after passing the obstacle.

Night Patrols and Method of Reconnaissance and Passing of Various Terrain and Physical Objects.—

1. Woods.

More minute care must be exercised with respect to woods at night than in day time. The following things, especially, must be borne in mind:

(a) Don't enter a woods unless unavoidable; on account of its darkness the field of view is restricted, there is sure to be noise, and it is unfavorable for hearing, so pass around the edge if possible.

(b) When about to enter a woods, first reconnoiter the interior; if possible one man will advance to the edge.

(c) While in the woods, stop from time to time and listen.

(d) When the passage is difficult, even though you force your way through, it will usually do more harm than good.

(e) It is important that one should always expect to run into the enemy.

(*f*) The principles already stated in previous articles concerning direction, connection, etc., should be followed.

2. Villages.

Villages are similar to woods, but the following special cautions are important:

(*a*) It is a good thing to avoid villages, as a patrol is liable to be molested by dogs, natives, or hidden enemies.

(*b*) When about to enter a village, first reconnoiter the interior from the outside; if nothing unusual is seen then it may be entered.

(*c*) One man should advance along the edge of the village.

(*d*) Sieze a native and question him concerning conditions; his attitude should afford some clue to conditions.

(*e*) While, at times, it is advantageous to sieze hostages, it is disadvantageous to arouse hostility.

(*f*) The patrol should pass along the side of the street in shadow.

With respect to the maintenance of direction, connection, etc., see those chapters devoted to those subjects.

3. Defiles.

If a defile is encountered in the neighborhood of the enemy, act in accordance with the following principles:

(*a*) As there is usually a hostile sentinel at the mouth of the defile, verify it.

(*b*) When about to enter, one man will be placed some distance in rear, and will follow only when the man preceding him has entered safely. At this time, the patrol leader will be in front, with one man somewhat in his rear, and the third man still further in rear.

4. Open country.

In open country, the following principles are applicable:

(*a*) Move with as low a posture as possible.

(*b*) Take as much interval as possible; in this case, the patrol leader is in the center, and guides both flanks of the patrol.

(*c*) Watch the enemy's direction, and put the ear to the ground and listen for noises.

5. Roads.

In order to avoid being seen by the enemy, march on the side of the road in shadow; if you travel in the center of the road, discovery is easy. The character of the road surface, and its relation to the amount of noise produced, must also be borne in mind. Therefore the patrol, itself, should move quietly, and listen for sounds made by the enemy.

6. Gravelly ground.

As much noise is produced while traveling over gravelly ground, special caution is necessary. It will be found disadvantageous for the whole patrol to move at the same time, and halt at the same time; therefore one man will halt, and the other two continue the advance, or they will advance in turn, etc.

7. High ground and depression.

High ground is advantageous for vision, but there is danger of being seen by the enemy when descending. When the descending slope is very precipitous, quiet movement becomes difficult; therefore, the patrol should proceed as on gravelly ground. When climbing to high ground, the patrol should halt at the crest line and watch and listen. It is a good thing, too, to stop quietly and listen, before crossing the crest line.

Night Patrols and Indications.—When there are suspicious indications, the patrol will lie down at once and listen. Its duty can best be performed if it is always prepared, and discovers the enemy first; accordingly it must avoid moving or firing rashly. As a patrol's movements differ more or less with the nature of their duty, we will discuss each duty separately.

(*a*) When entrusted with the duty of reconnoitering the enemy's outpost line. When on such duty, if a hostile patrol is discovered, the patrol will lie down at once and allow it to pass. Even though there are opportunities for taking prisoners, the patrol must not allow such side issues to divert it from its true mission. Its action upon discovery of the enemy's sentinels will be discussed in another place.

(*b*) When reconnoitering the enemy's outpost line, or the position of detachments in rear. The patrol advances as in the preceding case. If a hostile patrol is encountered while on the return journey, or after the weak points of the sentinels have been discovered, it is very important not to make any movement which will discover its presence and thus cause the enemy to change his dispositions.

(*c*) After the patrol has performed its mission, there are times when it is advantageous to try to capture or kill the enemy. However the patrol's prompt report must not be sacrificed for this purpose, neither must the proper opportunity be mistaken. A plan evolved from the prompting of curiosity or the desire for fame, is not to be commended. No movement should be decided upon without due consideration.

A Night Patrol's Reconnaissance of the Enemy's Line of Sentinels.—

1. Time for reconnaissance.

The most advantageous times for such reconnaissance are as follows:

(a) At the time of the sentinel's relief.

(b) When a visiting patrol passes.

(c) When a patrol returns.

(d) At the time of the arrival of connecting moving sentinels.

Such times are convenient on account of the noise arising from the movement, and from talking. Therefore, the reconnoitering patrol previous to this time, should have approached the line of sentinels, and have hidden in their vicinity.

2. Movements going and returning.

These movements do not differ from those previously made by the patrol against the enemy.

3. Methods of reconnaissance.

The patrol being hidden, as we have already described, it should strive to discover the position of one sentinel; this being used as a base will assist in the discovery of the other posts and non-commissioned officer posts. Having reconnoitered the intervening open ground, the enemy's method of security can be verified, and it can be judged whether or not it would be a good thing to enter the line of sentinels. To accomplish this, it is a good thing to follow directly after a passing moving sentinel or a visiting patrol.

Night Patrols and Quiet.—Patrols will not fire at night. If they do so, their mission will become difficult of accomplishment, and it will be harmful to succeeding hidden movements as well. Again, patrols will not talk—from this comes danger of discovery by the enemy. A patrol's halting, lying down, and hiding, will be without word or sound. There must be no double-timing, or confusion arising from lack of coolness or fear. Only in sudden danger, when there is no other means of escape, or as a substitute for a quick report, may firing be employed.

Night Patrols and Their Roads.—Night patrols will vary their roads in coming and going. If this is not done, there is danger of encountering a hidden enemy. If, on account of being on the return road, the service of security be neglected or noise be made, the enemy is liable to take advantage of it. During the late war, a patrol opposite the Shaho river, was in the habit of resting in a certain locality where the men would make a fire. The enemy discovered it, and planted a bomb there. For such reasons, it is especially important to return by a different road.

Night Patrols and Reconnaissance and Recollection of Terrain.—As members of patrols will sometimes be used as guides, they will reconnoiter the terrain with that object in view, and their memory must be trained at the same time. While this training is being carried out, the following points will be borne in mind:

(a) A base for fixing direction.

(b) The aligning and recollection of places.

(*c*) How to pass obstacles, and points to be careful of in so doing.

(*d*) The extent of the use of roads and neighboring ground.

(*e*) Special marks—such may be made as follows:

1. Scattering white paper.
2. Scattering white powder.
3. Breaking limbs of trees, or trees themselves.
4. Tying on white paper or white rags.
5. Establishing road marks or signs.

The principles governing the recollection of physical objects are similar to those under the section "Duties of Messengers."

XXIX.

NIGHT HIDDEN PATROLS.

Such patrols hide in important places and discover and report important matters; their movements, of course, depend upon the special purpose for which they are employed. However, under no circumstances, must they make their appearance rashly. The duties of hidden patrols although apparently simple, are not so in reality; success is more and more difficult, according to the importance of the mission. To simply order a patrol to hide at a certain place and only vaguely indicate their other movements, is useless. Whether it is to capture a hostile patrol, or to simply report the approach of the enemy, or to report other conditions (the enemy's movements, etc.), all must be indicated clearly and accurately. In many instances, hidden patrols will not be called upon to perform duties which other patrols can execute. On the other hand, there will be things difficult for ordinary patrols—such as the recognition of the enemy's night attack, maintenance of close contact, etc.—which must be entrusted to hidden patrols. In such cases, if the patrol tries to capture a hostile patrol, or if they go to the rear to report, their position will be discovered. A hidden patrol, accordingly almost never receives communication or visiting patrols from other bodies.

Suitable Characteristics for Hidden Patrols.—A hidden patrol, compared to an ordinary patrol, remains a long time in proximity to the enemy; its members must, therefore, possess the following qualities: Fearlessness, coolness, patience, intelligence and quickness.

Impetuous men quickly become confused and are not suitable for this duty. During the Japanese-Russian War, our hidden patrols on the Shaho river, though they did their work well, were sometimes taken prisoners by the enemy; but they did not capture any of the enemy's patrols.

Distribution of Hidden Patrols.—No one should know the position of the hidden patrol but the patrol itself, and the one who posts it. In this connection, the following points will be borne in mind:

(*a*) It is disadvantageous for the natives or enemy to know the position.

(*b*) Do not loiter about the position unnecessarily before assuming it.

(*c*) Remain in another position until dusk, and when it becomes dark enter the true position secretly.

(*d*) Other patrols or visiting patrols will not approach or halt at this patrol's position.

(*e*) When discovered by the enemy, or by natives, the patrol will quickly withdraw; it will strive to create the impression that it has entirely withdrawn, but later it will assume a new position.

Position of Hidden Patrols.—Although the position of a hidden patrol will be in accordance with its objective, the following points will be borne in mind:

(*a*) It should be a place from which important things can be discovered. For example, in order to learn of the enemy's advance, it must be in the vicinity of important roads.

(*b*) A place convenient for observation, but difficult of detection.

(*c*) A place not easy for the enemy to surprise.

(*d*) A place where the patrol can send a messenger or signal to its friends without being discovered by the enemy.

(*e*) A place not on a road used by the natives.

XXX.

TRAINING OF NIGHT PATROLS.

Training and Terrain.—We have already mentioned the necessity of training patrols on varying terrain. Both sentinels and patrols require such training.

Methods of Training.—

1. Instruction in the relations between sentinels and patrols.

(*a*) Preparation.

Having assembled the men to be instructed, the importance of this training will be explained. Distribute instructors and sentinels as in the sketch. The opposing sentinels will be at such a distance that they cannot see each other; in this interval there is space for patrols to move. Time will be wasted, however, if they move too far.

2. Orders for instructors.

Each instructor will be informed as to the points in which he will instruct his men. He will be placed in a particular position, and given the approximate time which he can use for one period of instruction. Such training will follow this general method:

(a) The instructor at B oversees and corrects the patrol's movements against the sentinel, and *vice versa*.

(b) The instructor at C acts in a similar manner to to the one at B.

This distribution having been made, a patrol will be sent out from the squad, first, encountering the sentinel's post A; after this movements has been corrected, the patrol will proceed toward C and B. The officer in charge will send out other patrols at proper

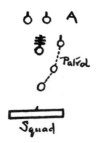

89

intervals, and when the exercise is concluded, will assemble the squad at A; then from the reports of his assistant instructors and his own observations, will comment upon the men's movements.

3. Secretly entering and leaving enemy's line of sentinels.

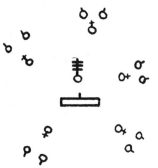

(a) Post sentinels as in the sketch; give them simple orders, such as, to keep on the lookout for the enemy, etc.

(b) Next, send out a patrol to act as a hostile patrol (they should attach a white cloth, or some other distinguishing mark); this patrol will try to enter the line of sentinels without being discovered.

(c) The instructors oversee the movements of both sentinels and patrol, and judge of the success of the movement.

4. Search for the enemy's line of sentinels.

Having posted the sentinels and attached an asssitant instructor to each post, have them carry out the usual duties of sentinels. Their position in unknown to the squad from which the patrols are sent out to search for the enemy's line of sentinels. At this period of instruction, two methods may be employed:

(a) Make an assistant instructor chief of the patrol, the remainder being recruits.

(b) Place an assistant instructor in the vicinity of the sentinels and have them criticise the movement, and furnish material for the officer's criticisms. It is important to limit the patrol's sphere of movement, and thus avoid unprofitable dispersion.

5.   Training when meeting hostile patrols.

The instructor, having divided the squad into two parts, attaches an assistant instructor to each squad, and places himself midway between the squads. He carries a disappearing light, with which he signals to both squads concerning the sending out of patrols. The non-commissioned cfficer in charge of the squads divide them into patrols, and sends out these patrols in the direction of the instructor. Each patrol will be ordered to return to its squad after they have reconnoitered the locality indicated by the assistant instructor. From his position, the instructor watches the movements of both patrols, and corrects them if necessary. When the men have had some training in this movement, one squad operates directly against another.

6.   Methods of training in how to pass and reconnoiter terrain and physical objects do not differ in principle from the methods employed in day time, which have already been explained.

XXXI.

MOVEMENTS OF A DETACHMENT AT NIGHT.

Leadership at Night.—We have examined, roughly, the natural qualities required of the men at nighttime, the next thing is the manner of leadership. The difficulty of such leadership at night, is beyond description. In turning our attention to this kind of training, one point stands out most prominently—quietness of leadership. At night, as it is important to avoid discovery by the enemy, the men under one's command must be a mass without sound—and this mass must move by silent leadership.

The value of night movements depends upon the amount of skill displayed in silent leadership. Such leadership is attained by the following means:

1. By signals.

These signals will be briefly explained to the men, and may be made by a saber, flag or light; in any case, the following requirements must be fulfilled:

(a) The signal must be clearly understood by the men.

(b) It must not be visible to the enemy.

There is no necessity for a great amount of drill in this kind of signalling, because night movements are seldom complicated. Such movements are the causes of failure, and simple movements and consequently simple signals only will be employed. For example:

(a) Advance—raise the object with which the signal is made, vertically.

(b) Halt—raise and lower the object, keeping it vertical.

(c) Lie down—Move the object toward the ground.

(d) To form parallel columns and advance—a circular motion, or several times to the right and left.

(e) To form column of companies and advance—A circular movement.

There are several other important signals in which

commanding officers will instruct their men in the day-time.

2. Method by relays.

The success of this method of silent leadership depends greatly upon the amount of training in peace time. When the voice is used, it is important that it be just loud enough to be heard by the neighboring soldier, and that the rate of speech be as rapid as possible. Although these methods can be accurately executed when the enemy is at some distance, there is always the danger of messengers making mistakes, and delay is directly proportional to the distance from the sender. However, in many cases, the formation at night being the normal formation in column of companies, neither the front or depth will be very great, and, if well trained in this method, success can be expected.

3. Method by example.

Soldiers move in accordance with the movements of their leaders; in order that this may be done, the leader must be in such a position that he can be clearly seen by his men. Then when the leader moves, the men move; when he halts, they halt; and when he lies down, they lie down also. Troops can be led comparatively easily by this method; and even though men cannot see the leader directly, they will be able to conform to his movements. The weak point of this method is, that timid soldiers unconsciously affect the movements of others. Therefore in time of peace, the characteristics of each man must be known, and the training must be done with minute care.

To Accustom Troops to Change of Formation at Night.—A change of formation at night is attended with various kinds of confusion. Even if this is not the case, it is difficult to carry it out quietly, and slackness is unavoidable. Therefore training in carrying out simple changes of formation quietly and without confusion, is most important. Special training should be given in executing the following movements:

(a) Column of fours to parallel columns—circular signal.

(b) Parallel columns to company columns—circular signal.

(c) Column of fours to company column—circular, right and left signal.

(d) Column of companieis and parallel columns to column of fours—front to rear signal.

In these signals, as a general principle, a circular signal means changing to a broader front; a signal from front to rear means contracting the front and increasing depth of column.

Individual Cautions in Movement by Squad. (See Night Movements of Squad).

(a) Not to talk.

(b) Not to hang the head during the march.

(c) To be careful about connection in the squad; each man will keep his place accurately.

(d) Each man will see that his clothing and equipments make no noise.

XXXII.

TRAINING IN SQUAD MOVEMENT AT NIGHT.

Order.—First, without arms, proceeding by gradual steps until fully armed and equipped. Very simple movements, as the advance, retreat, etc., will be carried out at first, gradually leading up to complicated ones. The signals should be learned thoroughly in daytime, and, later, executed at night.

Night Movements and Strictness.—Night movements, especially, demand the strictest discipline; because, when it is a question of life and death, the influence of darkness brings into being the animal love of life, and there is the fear that supervision may be avoided with consequent loss of power. At nighttime, therefore, slackness must not be permitted. Speed, silence, and strict discipline are essential, and the amount of training will be directly proportional to the degree in which the troops possess those qualities.

XXXIII.

A SQUAD'S NIGHT FIRING.

When Carried Out.—It is a very rare occasion when firing can be executed at night. Conditions must be such that the squad is already quietly halted and have made sufficient preparations, and, while in an aiming position, await the appearance of the enemy. During the Japanese-Russian War, night operations were frequent, but instances when the charge was executed with the bayonet, alone, were few. At the very shortest ranges, a fierce fire was poured in, and then the charge was attempted. However from the standpoint of the offensive, it is a great mistake to prepare for the charge by fire action; as a fundamental principle, the assault of the enemy's position must be made directly by the bayonet. Under really unavoidable circumstances only will an instant's violent fire be executed, and then, under cover of the confusion caused by that fire, dash in with the bayonet. However, if such fire action delays the offensive movement, it will do more harm than good.

From the standpoint of the offensive, however, it is a different matter. Knowing of the enemy's attack, preparations for night firing are completed, a violent fire carried out after the enemy has approached within very short range is most effective; and if this be followed by a counter attack, success often follows. For such reasons training in night firing is very important, especially in the case of small detachments, such as sentinels, non-commissioned officer's posts, etc. When they understand such night firing and make good use of it, they will be able to obtain very good results.

Important Points in the Preparation for Night Firing. —In night firing, the men must be prepared in all the following points. The angle and direction of fire should be simple, and the enemy should not be able to avoid it. The methods are as follows:

(a) Prepare a rest for the rifle, and in the daytime from this rest, fix exactly the angle of fire, direction, and position of aiming.

(b) Use horizontal firing.

96

(c)   Aim by a light from a lantern, bonfire, or other luminous object, or fire by reflected light.

(d)   Fix an aiming object near the muzzle of the gun (auxiliary firing).

First Method.—In many cases, prepare a wooden support; that is, in order to preserve the angle of the rifle, fix a fulcrum at front and rear, and from this obtain the angle of fire according to the range. (This is easily fixed by practicing in the daytime.) In short, provide for the two important points—maintenance of direction, and of the angle of fire. (See sketch.)

Second Method.—This method employs horizontal fire trained individually during peace time. The training will be by squad, and the following cautions are especially necessary:

(a)   Each man to fire exactly to his front.

(b)   Each man's firing to be exact.

(c)   The feet must not be moved unnecessarily.

Third Method.—In a small squad, the following expedient may be adopted: Change the day and night positions so that the enemy will appear on the skyline. When the enemy is outlined against the sky, firing can be carried out.   However, in large detachments, this method gives the advantage of position to the enemy, which they can utilize to our disadvantage when it becomes light.   However, in the case of non-commissioned officer's posts and pickets, good results have been obtained in practice during campaigns.

There are other methods; there is the firing carried out after having caused the enemy to appear in front of a bright light which outlines him clearly. Small bodies can use this method effectively, if they are composed of men who do not fear death. This plan, naturally, requires the fire to be lighted in rear of the enemy, and, of course, great danger cannot be avoided. Flaming shells may be fired, and direct aiming carried out by their light; at short ranges there will be a comparatively large number of hits.

(3) *(1)*

引金ヲ附着シ
前後ヲ一定ス

The trigger is attached here. Movements of rifle to front or rear are prevented..

(2)

一三四

Fourth Method.—An auxiliary target is placed in front of the firer at which he aims. Commanding officers must examine the sights strictly in this method.

Method of Firing.—Loading the piece after the enemy has approached closely, is the foundation of unsuccessful firing. Therefore officers and men must know the following things:

(*a*) To load so as not to be discovered by the enemy.

(*b*) Not to forget orders to load, or other orders.

(*c*) Not to discover their position to the enemy.

In order to accomplish this, the firer, of course, will load before the enemy's charge. The command for firing will be by signal, or in a low tone of voice. It the enemy hear the command *"Aim,"* they will quickly lie down and thus avoid the flying bullets which come at the next command *"Fire."* Actual experience in campaign proves this. In small bodies, the following mode of action is advantageous, because I have used it successfully in actual practice:

(*a*) Have the commands for aiming transmitted from the commander by soldiers nearest him to neighboring soldiers, and so on down the line (in a low tone.)

(*b*) The commanding officer gives the command for firing according to the size of the detachment and the rapidity of transmission; at this time, those who have not loaded, or those behind time, will not fire.

(*c*) After firing at the command, the men will load without any special order.

The above is simply an example, and must not be adhered to, blindly.

Night Firing, and Collective and Individual Fire.—
Long continued individual fire is not advisable, for it
discloses the position and range to the enemy. In
many cases, therefore, it is a good thing to employ
collective fire, thereby keeping the men well in hand.
Such fire has the advantage of dazzling the enemy's
sight by a temporary flash, and then relapsing into
darkness, and is thus especially valuable at night. In
any case, firing discloses our position more or less to the
enemy; therefore, during firing, strict watchfulness is
necessary to prevent the enemy from going around our
fire and appearing on our flank or rear.

XXXIV.

METHOD OF TRAINING IN SQUAD FIRING AT NIGHT.

Order and Methods of Training.—Train the squad in
horizontal firing in daytime; then execute it at night
against various kinds of targets. After practice with
blank cartridges, train them in battle firing with real
ammunition. It is often convenient to carry·out this
and other necessary training at the time of intrenching.

XXXV.

SQUAD NIGHT INTRENCHMENTS.

Mehtod of Tracing.—In tracing intrenchments at
night, the following methods may be employed:

(*a*) Advance as skirmishers, halt, and dig in that
position.

(*b*) Establish soldiers or trees as markers.

(*c*) Use a tracing line.

(*d*) Scatter white powder or white paper.

In whatever method that may be adopted, the commanding officer will exercise strict watchfulness, and when he has fixed the position, he will fix the trace according to one of the above plans. It is very important not to mistake the direction in night tracing, as there are many examples of ridiculous mistakes on the battlefield.

Methods Relative to the Line of Trace.—

(*a*) Method in which the ground is occupied in column of fours.

(*b*) Method by extension or deployment (in position).

(*c*) Method by advancing after deployment.

Although the conditions of the hour will largely govern, on a dark night it is an exact way, to form column of fours to the right or left extending to the markers (see sketch).

Night Intrenchments, Cautions for Individual Soldiers and Execution of the Work.—The above subjects have already been discussed at other places.

Method of Filling Sandbags, and Intrenchments in which Used.—In this matter, also, much experience is required. When sandbags are to be used, the following three squads are necessary:

(*a*) A squad to fill the bags.

(*b*) A squad to transport them.

(*c*) A squad to construct the works with them.

101

Of course it is advantageous to fill the sacks as near
as possible to the place where they will be used, but conditions often prevent this. There are various ways of
transporting the full sacks. Progress is most rapid

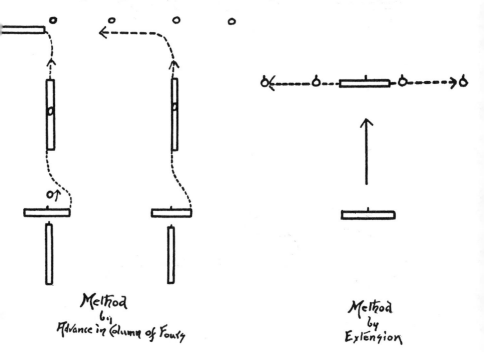

Method
by
Advance in Column of Fours

Method
by
Extension

when each man works steadily in transporting the sacks
from the various places where they are filled, but if the
distance be great, an intermediate station must be
established, and each man will put down his burden
there. Although the method of laying the sandbags
will conform to the actual conditions, they will not be
laid so as to form pillars, but will be laid generally level
like a skirmish trench by gradually progressing construc-

tion. In short, in this work, order, connection, quietness and coolness are required, just as in complicated engineering works.

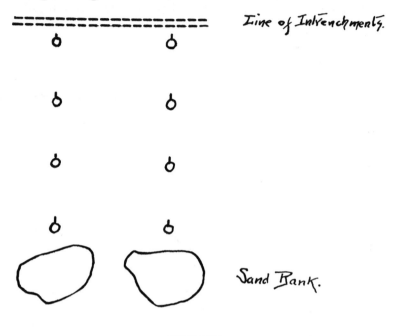

XXXVI.

METHOD OF TRAINING IN NIGHT INTRENCHING.

When the men are well trained in this work, the remainder is a question of leadership of the commanding officer. The order of training is as follows:

(*a*)   When the enemy is distant, training in the construction is the principal objective.

(*b*)   Training in the case of the gradual approach of the enemy.

(c) Training when there is fear of the enemy's attack.

When the above methods of training have been carried out in order, practice will be had in opposing an attack during the construction of the work; or connect this training with some drill in which they will use the works they have just constructed.

XXXVII.

TRAINING AND METHOD OF PASSING OBSTACLES AT NIGHT

Importance of Passing Obstacles by Detachments at Night.—My experience has been that often small obstacles delay the march at night; and these obstacles are all the more troublesome from the inability to judge their extent, etc., by the eye. On this account, training in crossing obstacles at night is most important.

Cautions for the Commanding Officer with respect to Obstacles.—

(a) He will inform all men who are to cross of the nature and extent of the obstacle, the preparations to be made, points where lights will be made, guiding marks, etc.

(b) Orders concerning method of crossing, formation, rate (pace), distribution, etc.

(c) Steps that will be taken to regain the connection that will be lost during the passage of the obstacles.

The above course of procedure will vary greatly according to the state of the enemy, the weather, and amount of light. Frequently, in crossing obstacles, the column of fours must change to column of files. If great distance is taken, much time will be consumed and connection will be lost.

Cautions for Soldiers when Crossing Obstacles.—If the men who have already crossed the obstacles try to regain the lost distance by double-timing, they will lose touch with these in rear. Therefore they should be trained in the following points:

(a) After they have been told what the formation is, they will maintain that formation while crossing the obstacle.

(b) When obstacles are encountered, if the state of the enemy and other conditions permit, word will be sent back to the rear concerning this obstacle, and a report made of safe crossing.

(c) The obstacle will be passed without sudden halts or starts.

In the grand maneuvers of 1910, a certain brigade of the Northern Army had to make a night march over entirely unknown country, and the road was only wide enough for a column of twos. On this road was a long bridge; when the head of the column reached it, they began crossing in single file. The troops in rear did not know the reason of the halt, and, although there were officers at the head of the column, the facts of the case were not learned, and the brigade fruitlessly waited the movements of the head of the column. Now as a matter of fact, the water was very shallow and easy to ford. On account of the darkness, however the men in front did not think of fording. Even though some soldiers who fell in forded it, they did not transmit the news, and conditions remained as dark as before. On this account the march was greatly delayed, and it was after midnight when they arrived at their destination.

XXXVIII.

NIGHT MARCHES AND TRAINING.

Occasions When Night Marches are Carried Out.—

(a) When executing rapid marches or forced marches.

(b) When a beaten army is trying to avoid pursuit.

(c) When attempting to avoid the attack of a superior enemy.

(d) In order to decrease the effect of the enemy's artillery; to use the darkness of the preceding night to advance to a point convenient for preparing for the attack.

(e) When about to carry out a sudden attack by taking advantage of the darkness.

(f) Occasionally used as a substitute for a day march on account of the heat.

Night Marches and Cautions for Staff Officers.—

1. Consideration as to roads.

(a) Complete reconnaissance, especially guiding marks, and repairs.

(b) Determination of methods of passing, going around, and removal of obstacles.

(*c*) Steps to be taken to prevent taking wrong roads, etc.

2. Consideration as to troops.

(*a*) With reference to connection.

(*b*) With reference to the avoidance of sudden halts and starts.

(*c*) With reference to the clear designation of detachments.

(*d*) With reference to the selection and alteration of formation.

3. Consideration as to security.

(*a*) If lights are permitted, the number of electric lights and bull's eye lanterns allowed.

(*b*) The manner in which the troops will be led—whether by trumpet, command, or signals.

(*c*) Whether or not smoking and talking are prohibited.

4. Considerations when halting or resting.

(*a*) Too great intervals must not be allowed while resting.

(*b*) Troops will not be allowed to choose their own places for rest.

(*c*) The men will not throw down their weapons, or other articles which they carry, unnecessarily.

(*d*) At the time of moving on, a rigid inspection will be held so that no men or articles will be left behind.

(*e*) The time alloted for sleep, no more and no less, will be used for that purpose.

Individual Cautions for Soldiers on a Night March.—

1. Cautions before starting.

(*a*) Clothing and equipments will be properly arranged and adjusted firmly.

(*b*) Care will be taken not to make any noise.

(*c*) Sleep during the time allotted for that purpose.

(*d*) Do not forget or neglect the calls of nature; do not leave anything behind.

2. Cautions during the march.

(*a*) Be quiet, and do not talk or smoke.

(*b*) Remain in the position prescribed.

(*c*) Maintain a uniform pace.

(*d*) Do not start or stop abruptly.

(*e*) Be careful about connection.

(*f*) Do not open out in ranks.

3. Cautions during a rest.

(*a*) Be quiet, and do not talk or smoke.

(*b*) Attend to the calls of nature, without fail.

(*c*) Readjust equipments and do not leave anything behind.

(*d*) Do not rest away from the vicinity of the stacks or the place ordered.

(*e*) Keep the haversack near the person.

(*f*) Do not sleep except when ordered.

(*g*) Do not drink an excessive amount of water.

(*h*) Do not enter any house unnecessarily.

(*i*) Stay with your comrades and mutually warn each other.

Night Marches, and Articles Carried by Officers.—
When about to execute a night march, the commanding officer will exercise the greatest care, and will only
move after complete preparations have been made.
Companies, without fail, will carry the following articles:

(*a*) Portable lights (electric lights, or some kind of
disappearing light).

(*b*) Whistle (officers carry these).

(*c*) Compasses (carried by sergeants or intendance
non-commissioned officer).

(*d*) Matches (carried as in (c).

(*e*) In the haversack of each non-commissioned
officer, some white paper will be placed, for use in connection duty.

(*f*) A small white flag or white cloth (officers carry
this).

(*g*) Officers will carry, or there will be placed in the
segeants' haversacks, twenty to thirty meters of string.

(*h*) In the belt of each soldier, about one meter of
string will be tied; it will be convenient in leading
them from the rear.

(*i*) Usually soldiers will carry a cap cover.

(*j*) All watches will be set at time of departure.

(*k*) Those who carry a sword will be careful to
prevent any noise arising from it.

(*l*) In a night march, especially when an encounter
with the enemy is anticipated, drum and fife will not
be used, and preparations will be made to use the trumpet
alone.

(*m*) All officers will carry field glasses.

XXXIX.

Night Battles.

(A) the offensive.

The Cause, of Success in Night Attacks.—

(a) All plans and distributions must be simple, and complete preparations must be made.

(b) The ground, the state of the enemy, and the weak points of his distributions must be known.

(c) Our plans and intentions must be concealed.

(d) Each detachment must be given an independent objective, and absolute uniformity will not be blindly adhered to.

(e) Our movement must begin near the enemy.

(f) Make use of the weather, move unexpectedly, take advantage of the enemy's inattention, and utilize any interval he may have left vacant.

(g) High morale, strict discipline, and excellent training are necessary factors. Also, firm resolution, quietness and coolness.

(h) The attacker must not allow himself to be hindered by any emergency, or by any action of the natives.

Causes of Non-success in Night Attacks.—

(a) Lack of the different causes stated above.

(b) When the defender moves on interior lines, and displays skillful leadership.

(c) When the defender changes his position before the assault.

(*d*) The occurrence of unforeseen contingencies.

Cautions in Night Movements (General Regulations).

(*a*) Things forbidden, and measures adopted for maintaining silence.

Soldiers will not load or fire without orders. Except when necessary, information, messages, speech, all conversation, commands, etc., will not be given in a loud tone of voice. There will be no talking or whispering. Men who have a cough, or who cannot see at night, and horses that neigh, will not be taken along. Take care that no noise arises from ammunition boxes, mess tins, bayonets, artillery wheels, iron chains, etc. Do not take along horses for light baggage. The necessary amount of ammunition will be distributed to individuals.

(*b*) Regulations concerning connection.

Attach white cloth or other easily recognizable material to the body or arm. Mutual recognition will be effected by countersign, signals, whistle, etc. There are other methods, such as wearing the overcoat, taking off the blouse, etc.

(*c*) Regulations concerning lights.

Be careful of the management of bivouac fires, the prevention of smoking or making lights, and methods of decreasing the reflection from the sword in the moonlight.

(*d*) Regulations concerning movements.

Make a clear statement of the objective of the march, the road to be taken, and the method of marching. The method of connection, recognition, the point of arrival, and what to do after arrival there (at such a time, it is difficult for the commanding officer to give commands; if the troops know beforehand what is expected of them, they will strive to do it.)

The Commanding Officer and Soldiers in a Night Attack.—

1. The commanding officer.

In order to be able to make detailed plans, it is important that the commanding officer have a thorough knowledge of the state of the enemy, his dispositions, etc., the terrain, etc. A minute reconnaissance both day and night, must be made over the ground where he expects to move.

The commanding officer must direct the fight, with a determined spirit. His position must be clearly defined, so that information, messages, orders, etc., may be sent and received. Although he must keep his command well in hand, after his policy and plans have been indicated, each detachment must act firmly and independently.

2. Subordinate commanders.

Subordinate commanders will strive with all their might to carry out the task assigned them. They must use their own initiative, in accordance with the plans of the commanding officer. They must understand those plans clearly, and must be diligent in learning everything possible about conditions which will affect their own movements, such as, the condition of the enemy, terrain, etc. They must see that, as far as they are concerned, there is no neglect about keeping plans secret, that regulations are complied with, that the men are kept well in hand, that connection is maintained, and that messages, reports, etc., are properly forwarded, etc.

3. Soldiers.

(a) They will guard the secrecy of plans.

(b) They will avoid panic.

(c) They will comply carefully with orders and regulations.

(d) They will maintain connection and touch.

(e) They will not load or fire without special orders.

(f) Even though fired upon unexpectedly by the enemy, they will not answer the fire, or become confused.

(g) When the enemy is encountered, they will strive to overthrow him by a fierce hand-to-hand fight.

Characteristics of Night Attacks.—A night attack, usually, partakes of the nature of a surprise; accordingly, it is necessary to gain success at one blow, by surprising the enemy. The plans of battle at night, are based on the avoidance of visibility; therefore, the attacker must press the enemy suddenly, and fight a hand-to-hand fight with the bayonet. At such times, a high morale must be united to a firm offensive spirit; because the panic of the defender is much greater at night than in the day time, and the overwhelming menace of the attack will derive a great effect from a sudden appearance.

Such being the characteristics of a night attack, great caution must be exercised to prevent discovery by the enemy, at such a time. When the enemy learns of the proposed attack, and makes his preparations accordingly, the attack will waver and the offensive spirit will become appreciably less. Therefore, noise and lights will be forbidden in night attacks; for noise warns the enemy's ears, and lights warn his eyes. However, sometimes the noise of a night attack is drowned by greater noises, as an artillery and smalll arms fight in another locality. If the enemy's attention can be scattered from the front to be attacked by such means, it will have the effect of a diversion; if, on the contrary, it only adds to his watchfulness, it had better be dispensed with.

At night it is easy to deceive the enemy, because of the confusion which arises from the misunderstanding of noises and the lack of vision. Therefore, it is a good thing to carry out a demonstration at the point the enemy expects an attack, and execute the real attack at a point where the enemy does not expect it. The demonstration alone will not deceive the enemy if it is so unskillfully made that the enemy knows that it is a demonstration; it must be executed from the beginning, just like a real attack. However, the false attack not being the main object, it will be modified as much as the necessity for quick reports requires.

Method of Night Attacks.—The great disadvantages of night attacks lie in the difficulty of leadership, and the lack of facility in the connection and coöperation of troops. Accordingly, methods of attack which require a complicated disposition, are seldom successful.

Although envelopment, in the daytime, is valuable for both its physical and moral effect, at night, its physical effect is decreased while its moral effect is increased. Of course this movement will be carried out whenever practicable, but its execution will be very difficult. When such a movement is attempted, a combined frontal and flank attack is required; but at night, this movement, also, is most difficult. Things go wrong, and often the movement is not only not successful but our own troops attack each other in the darkness. Therefore, when the configuration of the ground, amount of light, etc., render such a movement at all possible, the greatest amount of care must be taken to see that there is no collision with our own troops. During the envelopment, it will not be necessary for the troops to march a long distance in close formation; it will be sufficient to assume that formation immediately before the charge. In short, the envelopment which is of great value in daytime, is of little value at night. In the majority of cases, the issue will be decided by a frontal charge.

Night Attack, and Arms of the Service.—As we have said before, the conditions at nightime are entirely different from those in the day; so, in regard to the branches of the service, those must be used chiefly which are able to remove the obstacles arising from the darkness. Acordingly it is not wrong to say that night attacks are almost the special duty of infantry.

The cavalry, except when used dismounted as a containing force, will be used only for reconnaissance, security and connection. (There are times, however, when cavalry makes a night attack on the camp of the enemy's cavalry.) In other cases, its function in the night attack is to have all preparations made for quick movement at daylight.

Artillery rarely accompanies the attacking troops. However, there are times when it continues the day firing, or executes the so-called alarm fire by threatening another point; at times, too, artillery firing is carried out in order to deceive the enemy as to our plans. There are occasions too, when the artillery can assist the attack by a violent fire; but, in such cases, the necessary preparations must have been made beforehand in daytime, and the range must be short.

Machine guns are not directly necessary in a night attack, where fire action is not the main reliance for battle. However, when discovered by the enemy, or when fire action is especially necessary, machine guns have an important rôle. In the battle of Mukden, there was firing on both sides during the night battles, and machine guns, bomb guns, and hand grenades were used. Although, as a general thing, machine guns were used principally in holding occupied points, and for use after daylight, and were taken along for this purpose, they should be held with the reserve until the opportunity for using them arises.

Engineer troops are necessary for breaking up obstacles, opening roads, and for the fortification of positions which have been seized. It is especially important to have such troops during night attacks, as the destruction of obstacles in front of the enemy's position is chiefly entrusted to the engineers.

It is a good thing to have the other branches of the service carry hand grenades, and use them at the instant of the charge.

The Point of Attack at Night.—This point is by no means the same as in daytime. In the latter case, the approach is first made under cover, the enemy is then overwhelmed by fire action, and then destroyed with the bayonet. At night, however, the bayonet is employed at once.

As we have stated before, at nighttime, the relations of physical objects differ greatly from the daytime. Therefore the essential elements in the selection of the point of attack naturally differ; the principal points are as follows:

(a) The ease in which approach can be made.

(b) The shortness of the distance of the approach.

(c) The point where the bayonet attack can be delivered unexpectedly.

(d) Not only is it possible to hold the principal point of the position, but a point from which deployment can be made, can be held as well. However, a night attack will not be limited, by any means, to one point. With large bodies, especially, several points of attack must be selected, and independent attacking detachments will be used for each point.

The result of victory or defeat do not extend for long distances as in the daytime; therefore, a victory at one place by no means extends to distant points, and likewise, a defeat has less influence at other points. If these different detachments strive with all their might, independently, they will obtain victory. However, at nighttime, there is so much noise from shouting and rifle shots, that the original objective is liable to be forgotten.

In short, a day attack employs fire action to open the road for the advance; a night attack presses forward under cover of darkness. Therefore, it must be remembered that night movements are easy and secret, and that the cover which is convenient for approach in daytime, must be avoided at night.

Reconnaissance and Plans.—The principal factor in successful night attacks is complete reconnaissance. Detailed reconnaissance enables plans to be made properly. Those who plan as well as those who execute, must reconnoiter thoroughly. As far as possible, all officers should be well acquainted with the terrain and physical objects. If the officers who execute the movement are well acquainted with the state of the enemy and the terrain, it will go far in making up for defective plans, and will guarantee success.

Reconnaissance is carried out at night as well as in the day. It is very important to know what degree of relation the terrain and physical objects in daytime bear to those same objects at night. If this point be clear, mistakes and confusion will be avoided at night.

In a night attack, there must be such a self-confidence that success is never doubted. Such self-confidence is only obtained through feeling that the plans and execution are the best possible under the circumstances; and that can only be possible when complete reconnaissance has been made. The important cautions with respect to reconnaissance are as follows:

(*a*)   State of the enemy.

His preparations for security, and his distributions. (It is important to know, in detail, the position of the main body, covering position, protective detachments, sentinels' positions, etc.)

The enemy's strength, discipline, customs and peculiarities, also, must be known.

Obstacles and intrenchments. (Detailed reconnaissance as to kind, amount, extent, position, method of destruction of these objects, place, materials, etc.)

(*b*) Terrain.

Configuration of the ground occupied by the enemy; configuration of ground in front of the enemy's position.

1. The terrain as far as the assembly point and point of deployment; position of such points and roads to the front. The locality in which the advance is to be made, advance formation, method of advance, method of connection and communication, methods of removal of obstacles, etc.

2. Terrain up to the enemy's position. The apportionment of sections for the attack, distribution, methods of removal of obstacles, methods of connection and communication, etc.

3. The influence of weather and the amount of light.

Reconnaissance must be made on dark nights and on moonlight nights, in clear weather and in stormy weather, in order that the differences in such times may be clearly understood. Too elaborate plans are the foundation of non-success, but it must be remembered that simplicity does not mean just as one pleases. Often carelessness at the time of execution brings discord and confusion.

The Hour for Night Attacks.—The darkness can be utilized until success is attained; after victory, light is essential. This is in order that the fruits of success may be increased through the coöperation of the other branches of the service, the light facilitating the charge and fire action; it is also necessary and convenient for the reconnaissance of the state of the enemy and the terrain.

If it is still dark after the charge, it is most inconvenient for the succeeding movements, and is favorable to the enemy who is well acquainted with the terrain. However the time of execution of a night attack depends upon the objective of the battle, as follows:

(*a*) The enemy's position have been taken, if it is important to hold it securely, time the charge so as to be able to make dispositions for its defence by daylight.

(*b*) When it is desired to pursue the enemy after the capture of his position, the movement will be begun so as to be successful at daylight.

(*c*) When it is desired to attack by cooperation of all arms of the service at daylight, the preparations must be completed by that time.

(*d*) When it is desired, simply, to throw the enemy into confusion, it should be executed during the night, and the movement must be completed by daylight.

(*e*) Diversions, threatening movements, etc., will be carried out at necessary times, modified, of course, by the weather, amount of light, etc. After midnight, the enemy sleeps soundly, and the service of security often slackens. Therefore, under ordinary conditions, begin at midnight and try to finish the movement before daybreak.

Position when Beginning a Night Attack. (Point of assembly, deployment, etc.) In movements over long distances at night, connection is difficult, and it is easy to mistake directions and fall into confusion. It is therefore important to shorten the distance of such movements. To accomplish this, it is a good thing to advance the point of assembly, and deploy as near as possible to the enemy.

In order to conceal this place of assembly from the enemy and the natives as well, and to stop the movements of the latter, a covering screen against the enemy must be established. This screen must occupy the necessary points before hand, so as not to advance with the main body. If this precaution is not taken, the enemy will learn of the advance of the main body through the movements of the screen.

The point of deployment must be fixed from the conditions of the hour. The following points govern the selection:

    (a)   Amount of the enemy's service of security.

    (b)   Terrain.

    (c)   Size of our army.

    (d)   Degree of darkness.

    (e)   Weather.

In short, it is advantageous to have it near the enemy, just so that it will not be discovered, and in a place convenient for movement.

The British Field Service Regulations fix this distance at not nearer than 900 meters. If the ground is level and open, the assembly will be made in a deployed line at once, as a substitute for the assembly in column of march. Even when this is done, the zone of movement will be divided, and all detachments will advance in parallel formation. This is especially true when the movement for attack must be carried out from a long distance. When already near the enemy's line in daytime, or when already deployed near the enemy, the night attack can be begun from this line. The main thing is to make the advance easy by deploying as near as possible to the enemy without being discovered. The points of assembly and deployment, roads to the front, etc., will be marked as far as possible, by paper, rags, broken limbs of trees, or soldiers as markers. It is a good thing to block up the wrong roads, branch roads and unimportant roads.

Night Oders or Instructions.—Orders for a night attack will be based on the usual orders for a day attack· However circumstances may arise at night which make it necessary to violate regulations. The Infantry Drill Regulations say, "In the order for a night attack, there will be indicated the object of the march of each detachment, the road, together with the method of mutual communication, the method of recognition, and, if necessary, the point of arrival. Again, it is advantageous to indicate, beforehand, the first step after this movement."

If the order be made simple, it is especially necessary to supplement it by instructions. There are two kinds of orders necessary, depending on the distance to be traversed for the attack, viz.—the orders for the march to the assembly point, and the orders for attack. If necessary, both matters will be included in one order, or the order will be made as conditions develope. Orders from superior headquarters usually include both points in one order; the officer who is to execute the order, will divide it into two parts, and give the necessary orders. In the night attack against Kyucho during the late war, the men were told the general tenor of Major General Okazaki's orders; these orders did not differ greatly from the usual day order, but the principal things desired were explanied by instructions.

Distribution and Formation for Night Attacks.—The formation for the night attack must be simple. According to our regulations, company columns in parallel lines are used (line of company columns); or detachments covering from front to rear (for example, battalion column, or double column of companies). Sometimes a few skirmishers are sent in front, and sometines, not.

Although the line of columns is very advantageous as the greatest number of bayonets can be employed at the time of the charge, the movement is very difficult when the distance to be marched in battle formation is very great, or if the terrain is not very favorable, or if the night is very dark. The advantages and disadvantages of the battalion in column, are directly opposite to the above. The double column of companies is midway between the two above formations, with corresponding advantages and disadvantages; this formation is therefore most often used in night attacks.

However, the selection of the formation is largely governed by circumstances; each company must conform to the conditions of the hour in adopting the company column (column of platoons), or the parallel columns. While the latter has less masses strength than the former, the march is comparatively easy. Therefore, it is a good thing to use that formation while marching, and change to the other when conditions require it.

According to the state of the enemy and the terrain, the attacking troops, in depth of column, are divided into two or three echelons. Even when there is fear of a counter-attack from the flank, the division into three echelons will be made, the second echelon being placed in rear of the dangerous flank of the first; the third will be placed directly in rear of the first so as to make certain the success of the first line. It is important that the distance between echelons should be short. If it is believed that there will not be strong resistance at the point of entry, but that it is probable there will be a strong counter-attack after entry, it is important to make the rear detachments very strong. On the contrary, if it is believed that the enemy can be beaten at the first entry, the first echelon will be greatly strengthened.

Even in a night attack, a reserve cannot be dispensed with. If it is anticipated that the fight will continue until daybreak, an especially strong reserve is important in many cases it must be placed very near the first echelon. Usually, when the attacker's first line charges the enemy, its formation is broken up; this is true irrespective of the strength of the enemy. The ranks must be reformed at once, and it is the duty of the reserve to cover this movement and repulse the enemy's second line. The reserve, often, by an unexpected attack, can cover the retreat of the first line.

The Advance to the Attack.—When this advance begins, the troops must resolve most firmly, to be silent and quiet. If the troops can be led by signals and without the use of the voice, it is most advantageous. Each detachment must maintain the direction of the march accurately; to do this, the following principles must be observed:

(a) Select well defined marks, fix intervening marks, and follow them.

(*b*) Follow along roads, railroads, ravines, or edges of rivers, which prolonged, reach to the selected marks.

(*c*) Send out scouts; establish soldiers as markers, sign-posts, etc.

(*d*) Use military or civilian guides who are familiar with the route to be traversed.

(*e*) Fix the direction by compass, stars, portable electric lights, etc.

(*f*) Maintenance of connection. Each detachment will preserve connection and cohesion; unexpected incidents must be treated cooly; if the enemy's sentinels are encountered, capture them (without firing) or kill them with the bayonet, but it must be done without noise. In order to recover connection and order, halt from time to time. When each detachment has arrived at the attacking point, it will maintain order and quiet all the more, and will advance most carefully.

When the enemy's effective fire is encountered during the mrach, or when discovered by his searchlights, it is a good thing to halt temporarily, in order to decrease the effectiveness of the fire, or escape the enemy's vigilance. Care will be taken, however, not to retard the forward movement.

Night Attacks and Firing.—A night attack should be a surprise. However, even though the attack may be successful, it must be remembered that the enemy, when he fears a night attack, will take sufficient precautions and make preparations for fire action; therefore, never think that you will always be able to enter his position undiscovered. On the contrary, rather expect to be discovered; and the chief thought in your mind should be the necessity of a desperate effort in order to carry out your mission. The attacker must, therefore, be prepared to receive the enemy's fire; that is, he must be firm under that fire, and come to close quarters with the bayonet.

Night firing will not have a great effect if the attacker's movement is carried out properly; therefore, even though the enemy may open fire, it does not mean that the attack is a failure at once. On the contrary, success or non-success, depends upon the attacker's succeeding movements. For this reason the troops must not be thrown into confusion by this fire, but must quietly continue their movement. Silent intimidation will make the enemy believe that there is not a single echo to their fire in the darkness. It is of special importance in night attacks to increase the enemy's doubts and fears. If their fire is returned, the following disadvantages result:

(a) It discovers the attacker's strength to the enemy.

(b) It discovers their position as well.

(c) The enemy will discover the real front of attack, and will be able to make his dispositions accordingly.

(d) Silent intimidation loses its effect.

(e) It decreases more and more, the charging strength.

Therefore, by firing, the attacker destroys himself, does not injure the enemy, and the man who believes he injures the enemy by such means, is destined to failure. While in daytime it is necessary to open up a road by such means, when it is remembered that this is unnecessary at night, night firing will become meaningless. How much more true is this when the fire is due to the enticement of the enemy and is defensive in nature. One can say with truth, that night firing on the part of the offensive means failure.

Night firing by one detachment encourages meaningless fire at other places, and such things denote clearly the inferiority of an army. Therefore, the highest officer down to the private soldier must brave the enemy's bullets and long for the charge.

However, at times, firing is used to cast down the enemy's morale; this is only done when an entry into their works is certain, and is never done to provide an opportunity for entry or to open the way of the advance. Its functions is to increase the success of the charge and to dazzle the enemy, this purpose being best effected by the use of hand grenades. This is but the matter of an instant, and the attacker must already be in the position when the grenades are used; they will then rush forward shouting the battle-cry, and success is certain. Sometimes, firing may be used as a substitute for hand grenades.

Preparations Against the Defenders' Changes of Disposition.—The defender, in considering a night attack, takes the following steps:

(a) Complete preparations for night firing.

(b) Illumination.

(c) Change of position.

(d) Counter-attack.

Therefore, it is important that the attacker be prepared to take proper steps to meet such actions. Against fire action, as we have already stated, lie down temporarily, or avoid the direction of the line of fire. (The enemy's firing line at night, on account of the necessary preparations, is often fixed). If illumined by lights, lie down and keep still, in order not to make a shadow and to make the target as small as possible. It is important to avoid gazing at this light, for, if this is done, it will dazzle the eyes.

The defender, at times, will leave a weak detachment in the day position, and occupy a night position with his main force, and often this old position is attacked at night. When the attacker discovers this, he should make his plans beforehand, and not fall into the enemy's snare. The attacker should not take it for granted that the defender always occupies his day position at night.

When it is discovered that the defender is not in his day position, occupy that position with service of security troops, reform the ranks and scout to the front and flanks. Rear detachments should be called up, and emergencies provided against.

Sometimes when the enemy knows of our advance, he will make a counter-attack from a flank. Therefore, do not stop at simply providing for the service of security on the flank; make such a distribution that you will be able to oppose any emergency that may arise.

With reference to the destruction of obstacles, see the section on the attack on strong positions.

The Night Charge.—A charge at night is the penetration of the enemy by the power of combined wills and a high morale. This charge must come unexpectedly, and with an overwhelming impulse. The enemy must not be allowed to await our coming with rifle in hand; we must sieze the position in an instant, and must have a collected detachment to hold the position when the enemy, awakening, strives to resist. If the enemy open a violent fire and we stop to answer it, our movement will end in failure, and the movements of other detachments will be checked by the fire of one detachment. Therefore, no attention should be paid to the enemy's fire, but the charge must be continued without hesitation. To accomplish this there must be a self-confidence on the part of the commanding officer which expects success, and the subordinates must have confidence in their commander.

Movements after a successful Charge.—When the charge is successful, each detachment quickly reforms, takes strict precautions for security, provides against the enemy's resumption of the offensive, and pursues as quickly as possible.

When a position is once taken, it is necessary to make preparations against receiving the enemy's violent fire from every side as soon as it becomes light. Again, preparations for defense must be made very quietly. This makes it difficult for the enemy to plan the resumption of the offensive, and will make it difficult for other detachments to judge how to change their dispositions according to the existing state of affairs. Therefore, after a successful night attack, shouts of victory and noisy confusion, will disclose our position to other detachments of the enemy, and will be the cause of our being fired upon and re-attacked.

Pursuit After Night Attack.—Even though the night attack be successful, it is not good policy to leave the position suddenly and pursue the enemy, because of the many disadvantages resulting from the fact that pursuing fire cannot be carried out, the great amount of confusion, and the fear of receiving the enemy's counter-attack. It will be found difficult enough to hold the position, even. This is especially true when the position captured is only one section of the enemy's line, his other detachments holding their previous positions. In such cases, it is usual to make preparations for taking up the pursuit, and await daylight. When the pursuit can be taken up without fear of the above mentioned disadvantages, the success will be correspondingly great.

(B) THE DEFENSE.

Psychological Disadvantages.—At night, the defender has a feeling of anxiety, because the surrounding obscurity prevents the vision, which is so necessary to him. His principal mode of defence is fire action; and while that is very dangerous to the offense in daytime, it cannot stop the charge at night. Therefore, it is the duty of the offense to increase the defender's doubts, fears, suppositions, etc., and make a demoralized army more so.

For such reasons, the commanding officer of the defense must always strive to maintain good morale, quietness and coolness. How much more must he strive at night to force back the individual weaknesses of the individual, which arise on account of the difficulty of supervision. To do this, he must maintain a close formation which is convenient for leadership and which enables him to use the psychology of the mass.

The reasons for the difficulties of the defense are as follows:

(*a*) The difficulty of preventing the approach of the enemy by fire action.

(*b*) The difficulty of knowing quickly of the approach of the enemy and, consequently, taking proper measures against him.

(*c*) The difficulty of mutual assistance, on account of each detachment being bound down to its place.

(*d*) The fight is one of localities; other troops waste time (difficulties of leadership, coöperation, movement).

(*e*) The ease in which a defender falls into a feeling of being at a disadvantage.

Action of the Defense at Night.—On account of the above mentioned disadvantages, the defender must adopt measures to offset them. He must, therefore, take the following steps:

(*a*) Guard against the approach of the enemy by sending out detachments in front of the defensive line, by distribution of hidden patrols, by establishing electric bells, alarms, etc.

(*b*) Light up the ground in front, discover the enemy's approach at a suitable time, and make such approach difficult.

(*c*) Fix obstacles at important points in front of the position, and prevent the enemy from destroying them.

(*d*) Make preparations beforehand for night firing in the direction of the enemy's attack. Especially, provide machine guns at points where it is possible to enfilade the roads by which the enemy will advance, and make complete preparations for firing.

(*e*) Obstruct, by offensive movements, the approach of the enemy, and his engineering works.

When it is discovered that the enemy has approached closely and has constructed works, obstruct him by the attack of small detachments. The objective of such a sortie, of course, is not the same as that of the main battle which drives off the attack. It is therefore, not only not necessary to use large detachments, but when such are employed it is liable to give rise to a battle not planned for. As for the reasons for not always carrying out a sortie, all depends upon conditions as the time.

Steps when Anticipating the Enemy's Night Attack.— When the enemy's night attack is anticipated, have a formation ready to oppose him. Whenever the dispositions have to be changed at the time of the attack, leadership and movement are difficult on account of the darkness, and mistakes and confusion will arise. Accordingly, when expecting the enemy's attack, the following steps will be taken beforehand:

(*a*) Strict service of security.

(*b*) Place the necessary number of men in the firing line.

(*c*) Troops in rear should be called up near the firing line.

(*d*) Take necessary measures for connection and communication. (Distribution of lights, markers, etc.)

The Defender's Night Battle.—The defender, at night, will not permit a single soldier to leave his position. Each detachment will guard its assigned position, independently. Even though one section may be taken, no time will be wasted in re-attacking it by rear detachments. Detachments in the first line must remember that it is generally impossible to count on assistance from neighboring troops or troops in rear. The defense will strive to destroy the enemy by sudden violent fire from the shortest ranges. To do this, after preparations have been concluded, await the approach of the enemy; when he is very close, open up a violent fire, and throw hand grenades. At this instant, use the bayonet in a determined counter-attack. The enemy's random and searching are at long ranges must not be answered. Premature fire action causes useless firing to start along the whole line; it is not only noisy and useless, but it discloses our position to the enemy, as well.

At night, except for the protection of a locality, a delaying action will hardly be carried out. In this case, also, as large a reserve as possible must be kept in hand especially when there is the fear that the engagement may last until daylight; if there is no reserve then, the day battle cannot be continued.

Steps When the Defender Drives Off the Enemy.— When the enemy is replused, the defender reforms his ranks, but very rarely pursues with his whole force, as in daytime. Usually a small detachment from the reserve, or, at times, simply patrols are sent out (according to the French regulations, only pursuing patrols) who follow the enemy only. The remainder must guard the position firmly, as before.

Even though the defender is certain that the enemy's charge will be successful, he will not heedlessly withdraw from his position. This is because a night retreat gives rise to extraordinary confusion. A detachment which is pursued by the enemy, will again occupy a position in rear, and detachments not yet defeated, will remain in their former positions. Taking advantage of the latter's success, the defeated detachment will await an opportunity for a counter-attack on the flank or rear of the enemy who has penetrated into our lines. A general retreat, or a general re-attack, however, had better be done in daylight.

YOU WILL ALSO WANT TO READ: